From Vichy to Jerusalem
Memoirs of Hiding and Coming of Age

Cover: Map by G. Bergtrom; photo: Author at 3 years old

The Author and Translator dedicate these memoirs to all of their children and their families…, that they may remember from whence their survival comes, and never forget why this and so many books like it have to be written.

From Vichy to Jerusalem
Memoirs of Hiding and Coming of Age

A story of German Jewish refugees living in fear in France, of family loss, saviors and survival, of childhood, growth and learning, of Aliyah and destiny

by
Jacques Maurice Lévi

Translated by Gerald Bergtrom

BookBaby, Publishers

© 2022 by Jacques Maurice Lévi and Gerald Bergtrom
All rights reserved

Printed in the United States of America
First Edition, 2022

ISBN: 978-1-66788-329-8

Cover Design by Gerald Bergtrom

Jacques Lévi originally wrote this book for his children and grandchildren. But he soon learned that his story "resonates with others". The translator has included an *index* to help readers navigate people, places, and events in the book. To further engage with the author and the context of his story, readers can also use a tablet or smart phone, to access external links with *QR codes** to hear some of the songs that the author remembers from his time in hiding and in the freedom of his post-war years. To allow greater access to sight-impaired readers, a*lternate text* accompanies all images and photographs. Readers will find a *"Questions for Discussion"* section at the end of the book to guide study in e.g., a class or book club. For suggesting its inclusion and for editing the questions, I want to thank my colleague. Dr. Rachel Baum, a teacher of Holocaust and Jewish-American culture studies for more than 25 years at the U. of Wisconsin-Milwaukee.

*Please note that web links can disappear, even those for YouTube videos. But a *YouTube* or *Google* search should retrieve or find good alternatives to any that are lost.

Foreword

This memoire was (and is still) primarily intended for you my sons, and for you, my grandchildren. But I have been told, and since I started writing I have realized that my story resonates with others.

At this moment, now that I have lived most of my life, I see in it a surprising common thread, as if a guardian angel had been assigned to protect me from pitfalls strewn in the paths of all mortals, a protection that has led me unscathed to this day. Maybe we are all provided such a guardian, albeit each with different instructions. In these pages you will read the story of pitfalls and the survival in difficult times. In sum, the Lévi family fortunes were victims of the Shoah but survived despite the perils to which they were exposed. These included the four years my parents and I lived in Vichy France and the years my aunt Liesel remained in Nazi Germany and managed from 1933 to 1945 to stay safe from Nazi fury in the very den of the monster. There is nothing exceptional in this biography except perhaps the peculiar character of a destiny unfolding mainly in Israel, with no hint from the trajectory of my youth to predict the twists of later turning points. Though my parents would have preferred to keep me close to them in France, their second homeland to which they were so attached, neither my upbringing nor education predisposed me in any way in that direction.

Originally from Winnweiler, in the Rhineland Palatinate, my grandparents Isaac Lévi and Emilie Lévi had seven children, four boys and three girls, my father Walter being the youngest. Two of my father's brothers left no offspring; the third had only daughters. It was therefore only my father, the seventh and last child, upon who fell the privilege of continuing the name of Lévi with my younger brother and me. It is now my three sons who will continue to carry the torch of the Lévi. I would like to remind you that our Torah teaches that no territory was devolved to the Levites, who were solely responsible for the service of the Temple and the teaching of the Law. It seems to me, in the light of the errors of my ways and my personal data, that this is indeed the path of education that I should have taken. As it is, I did eventually end up involved in such service by successfully practicing as a speaker for over ten years. I am proud to recall here that the most famous of my distant ancestors was the prophet, Moses. May the life I have lived give you and others new understanding and perhaps even, hope, and may I have shown myself worthy of this life.

A Note from The Translator

It has been both a great pleasure and a learning experience to translate my cousin Jacques Lévi's memoires about his family's survival in Vichy France and how his life unfolded after 1944. My pleasure, the feeling that I know him now much better than I did when I saw him briefly, each time on many pilgrimages to Israel, comes from working with him on this project, and from the honesty and clarity with which he gathered his personal story and historical facts to write this book. My learning experience has included learning how to navigate the border between translation and interpretation, but more than this, it was finding out about the richness of a life (truly of lives) simply by trying to render this content in English. Yes, I read in French about how one could survive for so long the ever-present fear capture, torture and death under German Nazis and their French collaborators. But I came to know, appreciate, and love my cousin so much more thanks to the unstinting honesty with which he speaks about his upbringing under the shadow of the Shoah and the life events after the liberation in 1944 and the end of the war in 1945. Jacques originally wrote his memoires to be part of his legacy to his 3 sons and their families; thanks to our work together, this legacy is now also mine to share.

I hope that our English readers will experience and learn as much as I have about an under-explored dark corner of mid-twentieth century France, about the survival of its horrors, and about my cousin's remarkable life.

One more hope - that you will forgive any errors in translation; they are solely my own.

Notes to the Reader

1. A Family Chart

Readers may find this chart of those of Jacques's family members who feature prominently in his memoirs by name, nickname and endearment:

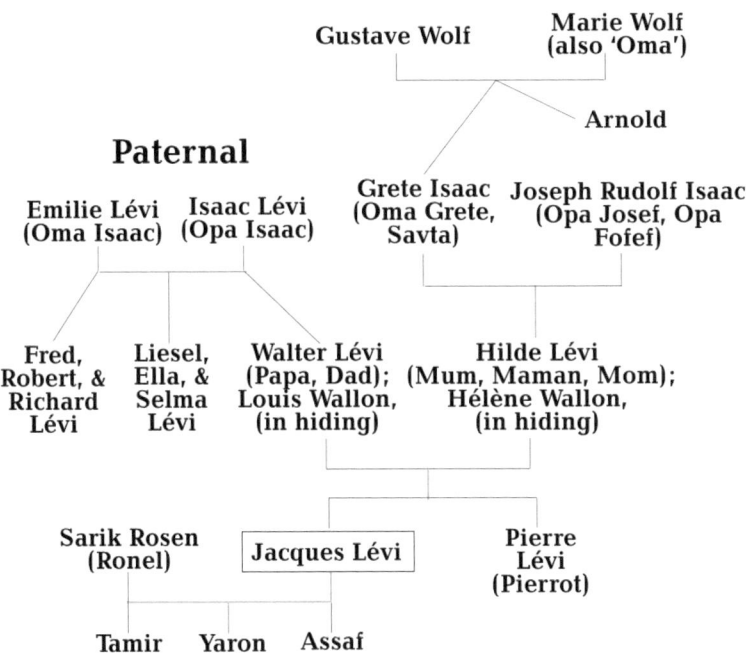

2. M. vs Mr.

The translator has opted to retain most of the French titular abbreviations (M. for *Monsieur*, Mme. For *Madame*, Mlle. For *Madmoiselle*...), in part to remind himself (and the reader) that most of the autobiographical and historical action took place in France, and to reflect the author's "mother tongue".

Table of Contents

Forward	v
Notes to the Reader	vi
1. A Family Chart	vii
2. M. vs Mr.	vii
I Come into This World, 1939	1
René Marcel	4
Some Words About My Father	5
My Grandparents	7
The Vichy Regime Arrives, 1940	13
9 Place des Célestins, Lyon, 1941	18
The End of the Free Zone and the Beginning of the Terror, 1942	19
Righteous of the Nations, Captain Louis Milelli, 1942-1943	22
The Righteous of the Nations (Unrecognized): René Marcel 1943	26
The Stay in St. Antonin Nobleval, April 1943-October 1944	29
Doctor Paul Marius Bénet and Heroes of the Resistance, 1943	34
Our Transition from St. Antonin Nobleval to Lyon, 1943	36
The Gracia Family	40
The Return to Lyon, October, 1944	44
The Municipal, School at 25 rue Pierre Corneille; Life in Lyon, 1944-1949	50
My Friend Pierre Charlet, 1946-1949	67
The Birth of My Brother Pierrot (Pierre), 1948	69
Our Move to 38 Rue Raoul Servant, 1949	71
My Return to the Sixth Grade, 1949	73
The Talmud Torah, 1949	76
I Am Last in Geography Composition, 1950	77
My Friend Alain Janconesco, 1952	81
Edmond Rivet, Teacher of My Second Class, 1953-1954	83
The Year of the 2nd Baccalauréat, 1955-1956	88
An Interlude of First Love, 1956-1958	90
My studies at the HEC, 1958-1961	93
Finding Israel… and Sarik, 1956-1967	98
My Time With the BSEL, 1968-1985	106
So Many Wrong Moves in My Personal Chess Game, 1961-1986	114
The Miracle of the KKL, 1987-2002	118
About My Work as a KKL Delegate for Legacies and Wills	127
Since 2002 and My Pilgrimage in France, May 2011	128
My Friendship with Christian Didier, 2011-2015	132
Questions for Discussion of *From Vichy to Jerusalem*	138
Index	141

I Come into This World, 1939

My parents: Hilde and Walter Lévi

The author at the age of 3

Historical chance fated me to be born in France, in Dijon, on July 13, 1939, to stateless parents, domiciled on the 2nd floor of 4, rue Alphonse Legros, while their roots for generations and generations were German. This is why, instead of continuing like my ancestors to revere Goethe, Schiller or Heine, I was the first to break the family tradition by becoming a fervent admirer of Jean de La

Fontaine, Victor Hugo and Honoré de Balzac. Although living in Israel for over thirty years, I have always been keen to preserve and develop this French cultural identity, whenever it is expressed in terms of beauty and humanity. These authors and many more are part of my spiritual garden. They are my fellow travelers, and their friendship has never failed me. When I entered this incomprehensible world, France was living its last days of peace and freedom. All those who followed international political news knew that Europe was on the eve of a formidable storm, the strength of which no one could yet foresee..., neither its duration nor consequences. The upheavals that occurred in Europe since Hitler had come to power six years earlier, especially in Austria and Czechoslovakia, must have worried my parents about their future. The violence of the anti-Semitic storm that had descended on the Jewish communities of these three countries at the same time as the savagery with which Austria and then Czechoslovakia were annexed to Germany should have convinced them to leave Europe at the beginning of 1939. Easy to say. Mum was already pregnant with me, responsible for her parents and for her own grandmother (in her eighties). This after being despoiled by the Nazis and expelled from Germany to France without livelihood. We were well and truly trapped.

As early as 1933, Mum, single and barely nineteen years old, had been sent by her parents, Josef Isaac and Grete Isaac, also German citizens, to Manchester in England where she had been warmly welcomed by the Jewish community. My grandparents, who lived in Grünstadt, had first provided for her maintenance. Then, under the influence of the Nuremberg Laws which robbed the Jews of their property and left them barely enough to subsist, they very quickly found themselves unable to send her money. Mom, who was playful, energetic, and pretty, was also endowed with initiative and a fashion sense. When pushed by necessity, she launched an enterprise creating and marketing of pull-over sweaters, eventually employing about twenty home knitters. At a time when women had not yet acquired their legal rights of citizenship, she had succeeded in becoming materially independent! Five years later she married Walter Lévi, my father. Had she not opted for the status of married woman, at the time incompatible with a professional life distinct from that of 'her man', there is no doubt that she could have had an excellent career as a businesswoman.

But feelings prevailed over ambition. Very much in love with Walter, five years older than she, and like her, from the province of the Rhineland Palatinate, she resolved to liquidate her small business and join him in Dijon where they were married on March 14, 1938.

It was on the night of March 12, just two days earlier, that the Anschluss of Austria took place, an event that was to weaken European democracies. Paralyzed by fear and made powerless by the impotence and incompetence of their leaders, they were vulnerable to the coming disaster. I do not remember that my father, though usually gifted with a keen sense of reality and sense of danger, suspected at the time that this event brought threats to the existence of the Jews of France in general and of his future family in particular. In fact, as he told me time and time again, emigration to the United States did not appeal to him.

My father, born April 1, 1909, in the village of Winnweiler in the Rhine Palatinate, was the youngest of seven children: three girls (Ella, Selma, and Liesel) and four boys (Robert, Richard, Fred and Walter). The last, although not included in the family planning program, was nonetheless welcome as shown by his Jewish first name, Baruch (blessed). His father, Isaac Lévi, my Opa (grandpa in German) Isaac ran a hardware store in Winnweiler that barely allowed him to support his wife, my Oma (grandma in German) and seven children. As a result, only Papa, the youngest, had the chance to study and was the only child to obtain his baccalaureate. After that, he had started his business apprenticeship. He was gifted with a fine physique, good looks, strong intellectual faculties and an unparalleled talent for mental arithmetic and for assimilating foreign languages. With a highly developed sense of social relations, he was very quickly deemed fit for sale. Before he was 20, he was already one of the best representatives of the Jewish firm L. S. Meyer of Pforzheim, which produced a successful line of silver and gold mesh purses for women. With Hitler's accession in January 1933, he decided to settle in France where he continued to use his talents for the same firm, which had moved to England. For four years, until his marriage to Mom, he integrated easily into France which was to become his second homeland and to which he was deeply attached. These years were for him a happy and carefree period during which he led the life of a happy bachelor and traveler, while consolidating his financial and material situation.

René Marcel, Part 1

René Marcel and Sophie, his young granddaughter

Here I must speak of René Marcel, a sales representative from Toulouse, older than Walter, whom the latter met and whose actions will prove to be decisive in events occurring in 1937 or 1938 in a hotel in Rouen during one of his representative tours. Papa, himself a traveling salesman, had reserved in this hotel, in addition to his room, the only exhibition room to present his collection of leather goods to his various customers in the region. Once he arrived at the hotel and after taking the key to his room at the reception desk, Monsieur (M.) René Marcel introduces himself, asking for the exhibition hall. The receptionist replies that it is not possible because the gentleman here (Dad) has already booked it. Seeing the disappointment wash over René Marcel's face, Papa then said to him: "Listen, there is a way to arrange it because I have seen the room and it is spacious enough to display two collections. We will stretch a net in the middle, so that our displays do not hinder each other." Surprised as much as delighted, René Marcel, who had noticed Papa's foreign accent, exclaimed: "So, that's nice of you, it wasn't a Frenchman who suggested it to me. At least allow me to invite you over for dinner tonight."

And this is how Walter and René became friends. It is thanks to this friendship, born of a small service, that Papa, Mama and I managed to survive the Shoah. This, in the most unexpected way, as we shall see later, proves the saying of Saint Basil, that "a good deed is never lost".

Some Words About My Father

My father Walter Lévi, outfitted as a mountaineer

I suppose that as the wise man that he was all his life, Papa succeeded in accumulating savings that would become a great help to him during the five years of Vichy Occupation. On March 14, 1938, at the age of 29, he buried his life as a child with some regret. Several times I heard him tell an anecdote about his honeymoon, which he had combined the almost obligatory *grand tour* expected of French youth. The tour had brought him and Mom to Marseille where he knew an excellent restaurant by the promising name of Lucullus. For a fixed price, you order a gourmet menu with no limit on quantity. The reservation for two having been made, how disappointed Papa was when Mum, whose stomach, already challenged by the rich feasts of the preceding days, asked the waiter for a salad and mineral water, which came to the table at the fixed gourmet menu price!

In his youth, both in Germany and in France, Papa was high-spirited and a bon vivant, denying himself none of the pleasures to which a normally constituted young man could aspire. Nevertheless, according to Mum herself, he turned out quite well! At the same time, he had played a few sports. These included football (which had earned him surgery for the meniscuses on both knees) and mountaineering. He (and I!) managed to save the photo that I have included here, where Dad appears in what I would call Aryan profile. He is in a climber's outfit taking a break, sitting on a rock. I have to admit he looks great. He was a brilliant conversationalist, an excellent bridge player (that he learned merely by watching seasoned players), and a more than passable violinist, playing without even reading notes. So, you can imagine that he was a much sought-after companion, particularly among the women..., with whom he had much success. I did not inherit his musical talents as a violinist and bridge-player and I have often envied him this past..., which I would have been more than happy to make my present!

Despite his Aryan physiognomy, Papa felt deeply Jewish. Though not very religious, his family respected most of the traditions. Immediately after the end of the war when our life resumed a normal course, there was not a Friday evening nor a Saturday noon, spent at home or at table, that Papa did not recite by heart the kiddush before and the *benschen* (or *birkat hamazon*) at the end of the Shabbat meal. I have heard it for more than 50 years yet never known these prayers by heart. Still their melody has rocked and resonated all my youth and reminded me week after week that we are Jews, and therefore different from the French around us. If by chance a non-Jewish guest joined these Shabbat meals, and especially if he was one of my comrades, a feeling of embarrassment, not to say shame, would wash over me. Clearly, it was inescapable that this religious rite would be a psychological barrier to the joys of my youth.

It happened sometimes when we sang aloud and in chorus parts of the *benschen*, that I would hear the voices of neighbors or visitors coming up the stairs and passing in front of our front door on the landing. That door was the only object separating them from our "dining room". I was certain that these people, who never failed to hear our song, must be surprised and puzzled by our unusual songs, and think us strange. At those moments I blushed violently with shame and would ask Dad to lower his voice. At least on one occasion, understanding my unease, he did not take offense at my request as I feared, but on the contrary explained to me, for once without impatience or anger, that I should be proud of our traditional songs. He even liked to tell me how, when his own father, my Opa Isaac Lévi, sang with my Oma Emilie Lévi and their seven children sang the same Shabbat songs in their house in Winnweiler, neighboring non-Jews (mostly Germans, and peasants at that!) would come near to listen for pleasure. Thus, Papa said that, whether by chance or choice, listeners to the songs we sang could not but be enchanted by the beauty of their melody.

So, you see, as a child I wanted so badly to be accepted as an integral member of *"the group"*, to be at one with *"the group"*, to blend in..., in short to assimilate. I wondered subconsciously why I had to be different from others since it only served to make me miserable. For all of these feelings I have blamed myself in retrospect. I think I had to come to Israel to finally stop feeling like a shameful Jew.

My Grand Parents

If I hardly knew my maternal or paternal grandparents, the fault lies with the advent of Nazi fascism which swept away so many nuclear families in its path, either by destroying them or separating and dispersing their members to the four corners of the earth.

My maternal grandparents were Grete Isaac (diminutive of Margarete), born 9/1/1888, and Josef Rudolf Isaac, born 26/6/1883. Grete was from Bad Dürkheim and Josef came from Wallertheim, both towns in the Rhine Palatinate region of southern Germany.

My maternal grand-parents, Grete Isaac and Josef Isaac, with their nephew Fritz Wolf

Oma Grete (Savta) is buried in my hometown of Dijon in a tomb that she shares with a foreigner. At that time in 1941 Mum was living alone and did not have enough money to ensure her a separate burial. Mum gave me a portrait of a woman who was not very happy, no doubt because of the marriage of convenience with my grandfather Josef Isaac, into which she had been forced. Opa Josef was an authoritarian who tyrannized over her and whom she feared. Oma's father Gustave, my great-grandfather, was away from home constantly and he died prematurely at the age of 54. While he lived, he hardly looked after his two children (Oma Grete and her brother Arnold). His wife Marie Wolf, my great-grandmother (I refer to her also as

Oma..., as Oma Wolf) had always shown a preference for her eldest son Arnold, leaving Oma Grete to feel less preferred, less than special. Grete had become a French teacher, a profession that she chose after a one-year stay in Paris before her marriage. In her relations with her only daughter Hilde, a child and then a teenager, she was a stern and very strict mother, attaching excessive importance to order, discipline and impeccably done homework.

Already handicapped by asthma (which I inherited), Grete died of cancer, too young and in great pain at age fifty-three, in our apartment in Dijon in February 1941. Her illness was just the outward, somatic expression of the moral suffering inflicted by the previous eight years (1933-41), starting with the daily persecutions in Nazified Germany, followed by the misery caused by forced exile and the theft of family patrimony. Add to these the feeling of being uprooted in a foreign land, the absence of any prospect leading to security, and the anguish of seeing all her family..., her husband , her only daughter, her son-in-law and her only grandson, me, having to face a cruel fate that threatened to swallow them at every moment. It takes little imagination to realize how she must have suffered.

In early 1939, already stripped of most of their property, my grandparents had pooled with other members of their family the little money the Germans had left them to buy an agricultural property in Morsbach, in Lorraine, just across the Franco-German border. They must have deluded themselves into thinking that the Hitler phenomenon was temporary and that they would return home soon. As fortune would have it, a year later in June 1940, this region was annexed by the German invader and the family was driven further into France, ending up without any means of existence whatsoever at St. Genis d'Hiersac in the Charente department, near Angoulême in southwestern France. The events of the last years had overcome Oma Grete's moral resistance and triggered the cancer diagnosed in a Parisian hospital. It was Mum with me on her arms, who took her to the hospital towards the end of 1940. As I write these words, I want to tell Oma Grete now of all the love and affection I would have given her then if she had survived. I know from Mum that Oma and I shared a taste for study, books, and art. I lost in her, besides the Grandma I so badly needed, a cultural guide of choice.

Her husband, Opa Josef (Opa "Fofef", as I am told I called him at the age of two or three) survived her by about a year. As portrayed to me by Mum, Opa was short in stature, self-taught, a brilliant conversationalist, much appreciated in society, but feared in his own home where he wielded undivided authority. No doubt disappointed that he had but a daughter as his only child, he had always considered Mum to be inconsequential. As a result, their relationship was never very warm. On the other hand, he had felt the keenest sympathy towards my father, with whom he must have found much in common. But Papa also knew how to command respect. As a result, it happened one day after Opa Josef had spoken to Mum, yet a young bride, in the harsh tone that he was accustomed to use when she was only his daughter, my father sharply rebuked Opa, pointing out to him that it was past time to address and treat "Walter Lévi's wife" with all the respect due her new status. In the short time he that knew me, Opa vowed to Maman (according to her) "to treat me with the greatest reverence". Dear Opa, even as a child I missed you, though I did not understand the reason or significance of your premature disappearance...

We had withdrawn to Lyon to be in the so-called *free zone*. But Lyon was in turn also occupied by the Germans at the end of 1942. Thereafter, the French police were charged by the Vichy regime to roundup and intern all foreign Jews in transit camps, then to be sent on to the Nazi extermination machine. My unfortunate Opa Josef was persuaded by a Jewish doctor that he could escape these roundups by being 'hospitalized' at Lyon's Grange Blanche Hospital. It was therefore in this hospital that he was arrested by the French police or the *Milice Française* (a special French police force working closely with the Gestapo) and directed to Drancy, just north of Paris, the anteroom of the extermination camps. He was then dispatched on the March 4, 1943, by convoy no. 50 to Majdanek or Sobibor... where he was undoubtedly gassed upon his arrival. He was not sixty years old. The doctor who proffered the unfortunate advice was also deported.

I was too young when my maternal grandparents passed away; I do not remember the slightest bit. Everything I know about them was told to me by my parents. It is clear to me that by murdering my maternal grandparents (Oma Grete's cancer was another form of murder), the Germans deprived me of much of the precious affection which makes all little children happy.

As for my paternal grandparents Isaac and Emilie Lévi, I hardly knew them at all. By the time I was born, they had obtained an "affidavit" (permit) to enter the United States and had finally resolved (almost at the last moment) to leave Germany, the country that was driving them away, robbing them of the possessions amassed during a lifetime of hard work, and depriving them of some of their children and their respective families.

Seated: left, Emilie Lévi (Oma Lévi, also called Oma Emilie, my paternal grand-mother); right, Isaac Lévi (Opa Isaac, my paternal grand-father); middle, Walter Lévi, to be my father (around 1929)

They came to take leave of us in Dijon just before their departure, which took place a few weeks after my birth. Mum especially remembers that Opa Isaac had blessed all three of us, putting his whole soul into this blessing, aware as he was of the coming cataclysm. Like so many others, he must have known that Hitler was about to send Europe up in flames and that Divine Providence would not be enough to save us from the fires on the horizon. Mum has thought about Opa Isaac's blessing many times since and likes to believe it was heard in high places.

When I truly made their acquaintance thirteen years later at my Bar-Mitzva (first communion in Hebrew), I saw in front of me a pair of old foreigners with whom I do not remember having exchanged so much as three words during their presence among us. My Oma Emilie was already suffering dementia. Of course, they were lucky to have survived, but Hitler had stolen everything from them: their possessions, their past, their roots, their full life in a pre-1933 Germany that they had loved before the Fuehrer's savage theft. Dear Opa and Oma, I want to tell you how much I would have liked to have known you, how I would have accepted and now return your affection. I miss what would have been your advice and your encouragement in the difficult moments of my childhood and then of my adolescence.

Sometimes I like to imagine that you, my five most familiar ancestors, Marie Wolf (my maternal great-grandmother, who knew me until the age of 5); Opa Isaac, and Oma Emilie; and Opa Josef and Oma Grete..., since you are no longer, and precisely because you could not take your place as my grandparents..., I imagine that you have obtained by way of compensation, the celestial power to be our guardian angels. The more I reflect on my existence and the various critical hazards of life that I passed through and from which I came out surprisingly unscathed, the more I feel that a protective and compassionate hand has brushed aside brambles and thorns or thrown a bridge over the chasms that threatened to engulf us. Perhaps without knowing it, I have from my ancestors the magic flute that their past merits have earned them. Or quite simply, if not a protective flute, then I have endured my ordeals because in the end, they existed.

Here now is what happened to Mum and Dad in the fall of 1939. In the days that followed the absurd declaration of war by France on Germany on September 3, the French army followed its defensive (and therefore its defeatist) strategy, limiting itself to waiting placidly (not to say stupidly) for eight months before starting any operations.

All this while the Germans had time to digest their Polish prey. In the meantime, the French *Ministry of the Interior* distinguished itself by interning in camps all foreign nationals living on its soil, particularly Germans and Austrians.

This is how my father came to be in the *Chambaran* camp (in the Department of Isère), after having entrusted Maman and me, only a few months old, to one of his first cousins, Ida Sternheimer, née Lazar. Ida lived in the castle of Montluel near Lyon where she behaved like a despot and terrorized her guests. The atmosphere that reigned in this castle was so unbearable that Mum made the decision in after a month or so to return to our apartment in Dijon (4 rue Alphonse Legros). By that time, my father had been transferred to another camp for foreign Jewish internees in Arandon, still in Isère. I will return to continue this history shortly, after a bit of historical context.

The Vichy Regime Arrives, 1940

On May 10, 1940, the Germans simultaneously invaded Holland, Belgium, Luxembourg and France and, in the space of a few weeks, swept away the Allied forces, plunging France into a chaos that is remembered as "le debacle". Under the terms of the armistice treaty imposed on France, it was divided into two territories, the *occupied zone* in the north that included Paris and, as far as we are concerned, Dijon, and the *free zone,* south of the Loire (with the exception of eight departments in the south-east, then occupied by Italian forces allied with the Germans.

On the same day as the German surprise offensive (May 10), Walter had been recruited as a volunteer in a British unit near Nantes. Six weeks after the start of the offensive, France was crushed, the English were able miraculously to re-embark for home at Dunkirk, while Walter and all his comrades abandoned to their fate. They had learned that Marechal (Marshal) Pétain had signed an armistice with Hitler. They were then given a certificate of demobilization assuring them free travel by train to the Pyrenees. Walter headed first for Toulouse where he had been dealing with clients. One of them immediately offered to lend him money. The next day on the rue René, he passed Marcel, the very man to whom he had rendered the small favor in Rouen that I already mentioned. Walter spoke first: "Aren't you the great Marcel?" The other didn't recognize him right away because Walter was still wearing the English uniform. Marcel said: "Take off your beret!" Then, in a flash of recognition: "Rouen! We presented our collections together in the same hotel". It was a happy and fortuitous reunion!

Walter told him that he had placed an advertisement in the newspapers along with thousands of others in search of their families and that, for this reason, had to stay a few days in Toulouse. Marcel then told him that it would take weeks until the announcement appeared and took Walter with him to stay with one of his friends. Meanwhile Walter had sent a telegram to his uncle Adolphe in Cleveland who at once sent him $50 by telegraph. He told Marcel that with this money he would rent a modest room so that he would not be in the way of Marcel's friend. But, changing his plan, Marcel definitively said "No way", and took him home! Marcel put him up in his son's room since he was away doing his military service.

This is how he met Madame Marie Marcel, a charming woman with a heart of gold. She and her husband said to him, "You stay here until you find your family, even if it takes years". In addition, he gave him a suit which belonged to his son and said with a laugh: "This way, I will recognize you more easily!" As you will read, Marcel was to do so much more - his actions were the providential intervention that saved our lives.

The new Vichy regime formed in July 1940 under Marshal Pétain's leadership rushed to embrace its anti-Semitic program publishing by October its racial exclusion laws against Jews, both foreign and French. From age 15 months until the summer of 1944, I was, like my family, legally indicted and publicly punished for the 'crime' of being Jewish. For those four years we led the existence of outlaws, knowing the fear of tomorrow, the anguish of being identified as Jews, of being caught, being separated from each other, being locked up in one of the countless French camps before being deported and finally, exterminated. This fear, of the slightest wrong word, wrong move, of denunciation, of hunger, of cold... was in short, a constant nightmare. Four years of that life that wasn't a life. It was a long time, a very, very long time. 'La France' led by one of the venerated heroes of World War I, Marechal Philippe Pétain, had by the laws above, refused the right to her Jews to live. Instead, she agreed to deliver them to the German executioner, starting with foreign Jews that had sought refuge in France. This is how 76,000 Jews living in the birthplace of the human rights of *'Liberté, égalité, fraternité'* (including 11,000 children under the age of 16) can thank France for their final 'right' to be exterminated.

Among the 76,000 is listed the name of Josef Rudolf Isaac, my grandpa Opa Josef, two of his sisters and a brother-in-law.

From July 1940, the Germans proceeded to ransom and starve France. Jews were among the most affected because of the discriminatory measures of all kinds instituted by the new Pétain regime. While Dijon was in the *occupied zone*, Mum managed to ensure that I did not want for anything. For her part, she remembers having suffered from vitamin A deficiency due to a lack of vegetables and fresh fruit. My father, demobilized in Toulouse, went to Lyon (both in the in the *free zone*), and then tried to join us in Dijon. But he was turned back at the demarcation line by a German orderly because he was Jewish, a foreigner and therefore 'stateless' even though his official home was at Dijon. This is how he must have realized that after the French defeat and the advent of Pétain and his *National Revolution*, nothing would be as before, neither for him nor for his wife and son, from then on.

To help her mother Grete Isaac (by then seriously ill) and her destitute maternal grandmother (Oma Wolf, driven out of Morsbach to St. Genis d'Hiersac), Mum left with me (barely a year old) to join them. In passing through Paris she was helped, comforted, and advised by Aunt Yvonne Steinberg, a step-relative (her brother Oscar was the husband of Aunt Ella, Papa's older sister). Aunt Steinberg was an energetic woman of whom I will speak again later.

Seeing the alarming state of Oma Grete, Aunt Yvonne, whose two sons Armand and Robert are doctors in Paris, persuaded Mum to bring her mother back for consultation at the Necker hospital. There and then, Oma Grete would be diagnosed with generalized, terminal cancer. With this sad prospect, Mom brought them back to Dijon. Her mother and grandmother will stay with us in the small apartment on rue Alphonse Legros while Opa Joseph will stay with Mum's friends. This is Mum's narrative of this time under the Vichy:

I learned that Walter was at the time in Lyon, trying to cross the demarcation line to join us in Dijon. You couldn't officially post letters, but there were opportunities to smuggle them. This is how I knew he had been turned back during an attempt to cross the line at Chalon-sur-Saône. Here is what happened:

When Walter reached Chalon, at the demarcation line, he ran into the German checkpoint. "Papers please!" Walter handed his ID card to the orderly. Although he read Lévi's name, he was not sure he was dealing with a Jew, as Walter did not have a Jewish physique at all. He turned the page and read: Father's name, Isaac Lévi. Really, there could be no more doubt and he began to shout: "Jew! Outside!" Walter tried to explain that he was going to Dijon to see his dying mother. "I'm not interested - get the hell away from me!" Many more people, Jews and non-Jews, whose papers were not in order crowded onto the station platform. Walter wondered with some anguish what would happen now. In fact, it was still in 1940. The only measures taken were to lock people in the waiting room until the arrival of the train from Paris so that they could be sent back to Lyon. Therefore, I resolved to obtain a travel permit as soon as possible to move to Lyon. Walter wrote me telling me to stay with my mother as long as she was alive. Day by day, her condition worsened, and people wished that the poor woman would be finally free from her suffering. Thankfully, it was not much longer before she left us forever. It was a true relief for the family, although the pain of the separation was very hard.

As I noted earlier, when Oma Grete died in 1941, she was buried together with a coreligionist in the same tomb in Dijon's Jewish Cemetery. In 1992 or 1993 I finally visited Oma's tomb.

After the funeral Mum decided to try to cross the demarcation line to join my father in Lyon. While the

German police made no move to prevent her crossing, the French gendarme felt it necessary to tell her: "If you weren't in mourning with a child in your arms, I would have sent you to Gurs". It should be understood that Maman, not being French but Jewish of German origin, could have been interned in the camp at Gurs at the whim of such an official. The Gurs internment camp, located near the Pyrenees in the region of Pau, was the dumping ground for thousands of foreign Jews, especially those of Baden and Alsace. Considering what happened to more than 20,000 Jewish internees in Gurs between 1942 and 1943, you will appreciate that our lives at that moment were hanging by a thread.

This extreme precariousness was to manifest itself several more times in dramatic fashion, and for us and for many other survivors, it is a miracle that we came out of all these ordeals relatively unscathed. It was not until much later, after much reading, watching films, and reviewing historical documents, that I was able to make some sense of this miracle, though if I am honest, it is still beyond my comprehension.

When, by force of my imagination, I reconstruct certain episodes of these dangerous times, I take turns feeling fright and dread, anger or revolt. Dread because I know only too well what would have happened to us in the event of capture and fright because what could have begun with just a moment of forgetfulness or betrayal; anger because the stupidity, indifference or just plain evil of zealous officials that could have destroyed us; and revulsion at a plague which blindly engulfed six million human beings simply because they were born Jews. And, each time, I stay prostrate and ask myself again and again: "Why them? Why not me? What good is this world where such wickedness is rife?

Returning to the events I must relate, Mom manages to reach Lyon without incident, leaving her father Josef and her grandmother, Oma Marie Wolf, in Dijon. As Josef did not get along with his mother-in-law, it was not long before he sent her alone, despite her old age, by train to Lyon, to join us. Still, finally, Josef later joined us in his turn.

9 Place des Célestins, Lyon, 1941

So it was that around March of 1941 that the five of us (Papa, Maman, Oma Emilie, Oma Wolf, Opa Josef and I) settled down in Lyon in what was at the time still the *free zone*. We lived at 9, Place des Célestins in a 2nd floor, courtyard side, 2-room apartment without a bathroom. Being of an early design, the toilet beside the kitchen did not flush. On the ground floor there was a Jewish butcher named Talheimer, a former cattle dealer. On the first floor was the Milelli family, originally from Corsica. He was an infantry captain. On the 3rd floor lived Doctor Charles Franck who remained our family doctor until after the war, and whose professional conscience saved me from severe appendicitis years later, when I was turning seventeen. On the 4th floor lived a Jewish couple, the Judax with their adopted daughter Liliane.

Even in the spring of 1941, already under Vichy racial laws, we ran the risk of possible internment in one of the French camps reserved for foreign Jews. My parents had "stateless" status in France even though, having been born in France, I was French. It was probably to escape our fate that my father had taken steps to obtain an entry visa to the United States for the five of us. This visa was granted to my parents and to me only. A solution remained to be found for Oma Wolf and Opa Josef, who in the meantime had found an activity (call it work if you like) negotiating scraps of fabric to tailors. Papa eventually succeeded in placing Oma in a Catholic religious establishment in Montplaisir, a district of Lyon. This assured her a measure of protection, in return for payment of course. I don't know what solution he had planned for Opa, no doubt also at his expense. In any case, the attack on Pearl Harbor in December 1941 triggered the entry of the United States into war with Japan, Germany and Italy, voiding any chances of immigration to the United States. Indeed, Vichy France, which had been engaged in collaboration with Germany, also severed all diplomatic relations with the United States.

The trap was closing in on us…

On January 20, 1942, the decision to implement the final solution was reached at the conference of Gross Wannsee, a suburb of Berlin. In March, just two months later, began the annihilation of European Judaism. The first deportations of Jews were from occupied France, with priority given to foreign Jews. I am sure that this alarming news quickly reached my father, even in a time when radio was censored. I assume also that my parents felt most threatened at this time, even though we were living in the *free zone*. Seven months later, on November 8, the Allies (Americans and English) landed in North Africa at Algiers. The Germans entered and occupied the *free zone* two days later. From November 10, 1942, our capture was only a matter of time.

I spent most of my youth in Lyon except for the 18 months from March 1943 to October 1944. It was then that with forged identity papers and fear of capture, we fled Lyon and went in to hiding in St. Antonin Nobleval, a small village in Tarn-et-Garonne. When the alarm had passed, we were able to return to Lyon. I will say more about this hiatus of refuge and the aforementioned Milleli family later.

The End of the 'Free Zone' and The Beginning of the Terror, 1942

By the second week of November 12, 1942, the Germans settled in Lyon. Among them was Klaus Barbie, head of the Gestapo. Gestapo headquarters were distributed in several places: at the Terminus hotel next to Perrache station; in a building at the corner of place Bellecour and rue Alphonse Fochier where torture was carried out; and at the Santé Militaire school on the avenue Berthelot, now transformed into a Museum of the Resistance and Deportation. This sinister building was commemorated in the excellent film by Jean-Pierre Melville (whose real name is Grumbach) called "The Army of Shadows", whose main actors include Paul Meurisse, Simone Signoret and Lino Ventura. The Gestapo's task was to track down resistance fighters and Jews. The latter were promised pre-trial detention at Fort Montluc, in the heart of Lyon, in the "Jewish hut" before being transported to Drancy and, from there, to Auschwitz. At that time, few had heard of Auschwitz, but everyone was aware of a mortal danger. The risk was not only represented by the Germans, but also by the French. Jews lived in fear of French anti-Semites, whistleblowers in search of financial or in-kind gain, the Vichy police, and finally, from January 1943, the formidable Vichy paramilitary *Milice Française* (French Militia). The latter in league with the Gestapo... and often crueler. Thereafter, the daily anguish aroused by the constant fear of an arrest in the street, of a sudden raid in a public place (cafes, cinemas, even shops), or of the ringing of the apartment doorbell, turned life into a permanent nightmare.

Mum remembers being with Dad in a cafe one day during such a raid. Some men in civilian clothes walked into the cafe sharply shouting: "Identity check. Present your papers!" My parents presented theirs (under the names of Hélène and Louis Wallon). Mum knows that her grandmother, Oma Wolf, is at home with me, awaiting her return. What will become of them if Walter and Hilde are arrested? In the event of an interrogation, Mom's still uncertain knowledge of French will flag her right away as a foreigner, as a German. If suspected of being a refugee and no doubt a Jewess, then and there, the whole family is gone. The seconds it took for a man to read papers and decide to return them must have seemed like an eternity to my parents. They came out of the cafe in one piece, undamaged, their legs shaky, still overwhelmed by the peril they had just escaped. This time, once again, they got away with it. Until the next alert. What are their chances of surviving in such conditions? If God exists, there is no one left to help them. Every mention of this memory brings back to Mum the horrible feeling of panic that seized her then.

During a vacation we spent in Arlanc in 1941, my parents met a childless couple from Lyon, Joseph and Louise Pélisson, at the hotel; they had developed some affection for me. M. Pélisson held a managerial position at the SNCF (the French national state-owned railway company) and so, was always aware of the actions of the Germans and the Vichy police. Knowing the precariousness of our situation, Joseph had left his contact details to my father in case of necessity. As the situation of Jews in France worsened further in 1943 with the entry of the *Milice Française*, my father contacted Joseph Pélisson to express his concerns. Joseph had two elderly aunts, sisters named Charlotte and Elise, who lived together in a modest apartment on the top floor of 33, quai Saint-Antoine in Lyon. On March 14, 1943, having heard that a roundup of Jews was brewing in our neighborhood, Joseph Pélisson went to my parents at night to advise them to go and spend a few nights with his aunts until calm returned, adding: "I myself am risk being arrested". I have very vague memories of those brave aunts whom we saw several times after the Liberation. They would sing songs to me or tell me stories.

All of these people took pity on us and did their best to protect us when it was strictly forbidden under the most severe penalties to come to the aid of Jews. May the memory of the Pélissons and their good aunts be blessed forever!

Since January 1943, because of the reign of terror of the formidable Militia, this Gestapo auxiliary, the situation in Lyon had become untenable. The noose was tightening every day. Opa Josef had left our apartment to take refuge at Grange Blanche Hospital, no doubt on the advice of a doctor, also a refugee. As I wrote earlier, this was a fatal decision. Immediately identified as a German Jewish refugee upon admission to hospital, he was arrested by the police and interned in Montluc. Papa tried to intervene by calling the Palais de Justice where the Vichy police were stationed. The manager who received the communication then said, "What's your stepfather's name?" "Josef Rudolf Isaac". The official replied brutally: "He will do like the others!" And hung up. Papa had succeeded in placing Oma in the convent in Monplaisir, a district of Lyon.

Now that we had to leave Lyon. Papa managed to obtain false papers. For this we had to choose a new and very French name, and for this there was a problem - all Papa's shirts were marked with his initials, WL (Walter). The trouble is that there was at the time, no French first name that began with a W. So, this was how it was decided then, that the patronymic would be Wallon and the first name Louis. Mom became Hélène. But the false papers were not enough. A false military file was now necessary to 'prove' that the said Louis Wallon had served in a French military unit. It was at this moment that Providence once again came to our aid in the person of our neighbor on the first floor, the Corsican Captain Louis Milelli.

The Righteous of the Nations, Captain Louis Milelli, 1942-1943

The Corsican Captain, Louis Milelli

The facts that I am going to relate took place between the end of 1942 and April 1943 when my parents and I (then aged 3), lived on the 2nd floor of 9, Place des Célestins in Lyon - this address is crucial for an understanding the story. To understand the context of this period, it is also necessary to remind you that right after November 10, 1942, date on which the Anglo-American Allies landed in North Africa, the German army crossed the line of demarcation and occupied all the French territory. The Gestapo arrived with the army and began hunting down the Jews in what had been the *free zone*, with a view to their deportation. France collaborated willingly and very effectively in this hunt through the paramilitary *Milice Française*, created by the Vichy government on January 30, 1943. The Jews now experienced constant anguish, day and night. This deadly threat took on various forms, some more hideous than the others: the constant prospect of suddenly hearing violent punches delivered by the 'gestapoists' at the door of the house, the sudden raids on café terraces, at the exits of cinema or, simply, in the middle of the street. At night, if we fell asleep at all, it was to wake up the next morning with fear in our stomachs. My mother told me several times that she was so deeply traumatized by this situation, that at the height of this infernal nightmare her late mother (who had died earlier), appeared to her one night in a dream and said to her: "Don't be afraid, my child, no harm will happen to you ". Maybe it was only a dream, but it came at the right time.

So it was that at the beginning of 1943, my father knew that we had to leave Lyon as soon as possible, and that we had to "go underground" and assume a false name, since too many people there knew us under our name of Lévi. We were at the mercy of denunciation under the slightest pretext, most commonly a profit motive since this was a time of scarcity; Denunciation could reward the denouncer such rare commodities as butter or sugar. As I wrote earlier, my father was able to get hold of fake ID cards, but he was still missing that fake military record.

Providence came to his aid in the person of our neighbor, Louis Milelli, a Corsican infantry captain of the 99th Infantry Regiment (IR). He agreed to arrange for the necessary false military identity for my father without asking for financial compensation (which as my mother points out in her account, was remarkable during this time of severe shortages). According to the false military record created by Captain Milelli, my father was "assigned" to the same, his own 99th IR. The captain was thus taking a huge risk because if my parents had been detained and the police chose to investigate false military documents, the origin of the forgery would have quickly led straight to Captain

Milelli. Helping Jews was by then a well-known and serious offense that carried the punishment of deportation and death. The captain further added to his "offense" by arranging to have my parents' fake ID cards authenticated by the local police station. It was thanks to the Good Captain that we were able to leave Lyon under our new identity around April 1943 to take refuge in a village in the southwest, as it turns out, narrowly escaping deportation and death. You will understand more fully the desperate fear of my parents when you realize that upon their return to Lyon after the liberation of the city at the end of 1944, they learned of their denunciation by the district baker's son. He was a militiaman. The Gestapo (or the Militia) had in fact come to apprehend us a day or two after our flight.

All these facts are in among my mother's memoirs which she wrote in German (her mother tongue) after the end of the war. I had read it while still young, not appreciating that the actions of Captain Louis Milelli were nothing short of heroic. Moreover, I read Maman's memoire before 1962, the year that *Righteous of the Nations* began to be honored by the Yad Vashem institution. And I was not as aware of the history of the Holocaust as I later became. It was only quite recently, in 2005, when I had left Israel on a temporary basis to come and help my mother in Lyon because of her state of health that I decided to translate my mother's memoires into French. I did so for the sake of my sons. Having arrived at the episode of the Corsican captain, I then took in, for the first time, the full measure of the perilous risk that this providential man had taken in acting according to the dictates of his conscience. I then felt the urgent need to find our hero's trail. But sixty-two years had already passed since these tragic events.

My mother, in her account, had spelled the captains name as "Milleli". The captain had in all probability already died and apart from his surname and military rank, I knew absolutely nothing about his family. I checked the Rhône telephone directory on the off chance that his surname was listed there, but there was no one under that name. Then I remembered that he was of Corsican origin, so I searched the Internet white pages for telephone numbers on Corsica listed with the name "Milleli". A similar surname spelled

"Milelli" appeared twenty-seven times on my screen and "Milleli" only once! I mentally prepared to phone each of them, trying to think about how I would introduce myself and how I would explain why I was calling. I called the first on the list and by chance it was the only one spelled "Milleli," as my mother had spelled it. The voice of a young man answered me. I was incredibly lucky. These are approximately the words of the interview:

Me: "Hello, I am calling you from Lyon to find the traces of a gentleman bearing your name who, during the years of WWII, served with the rank of captain in the Army and lived in Lyon."
Him: "Indeed, Louis, my grandfather, actually served as captain in the 99th Infantry Regiment stationed in the Lyon region and resided in Lyon."
Me (very tense): "Do you know at what address exactly?"
Him: "9, Place des Célestins."
Me (stunned): "Gosh, that's amazing!" Is he still alive? "
Him: "No, he passed away over twenty years ago."
Me: "And your father?"
Him: "Alas, he also died prematurely"
Me: "Of the twenty-seven Milellis I found in the phone book, are you the only one whose surname is spelled Milleli?
Him: "not at all, the name is Milelli like all the others it is probably a mistake of the Post".

This "mistake" had providentially put me on the trail of the good Milelli right from the start! I then explained to his grandson the reason for my call, expressing to him the joy felt at having found the traces of his grandfather.

On the same day of this interview, in August 2005, I reported to my mother the results of my research and my interview with the grandson of our rescuer, she was deeply moved. Together we made the decision to start proceedings with Yad Vashem for the posthumous award of the Righteous Nations Medal to Louis MILELLI, blessed be his memory. For my part, I am very happy that my mother had the opportunity to sign at the bottom of the testimony relating the act of rescue of Corsican captain Louis MILELLI in order to return to the latter the homage that is due to him. My mother died just a few weeks later.

The ceremony took place in presence of the Consul of Israel in Marseilles and the Regional Delegate of Yad Vashem in Nice on November 20, 2007.

Presentation of the Medal of the Righteous to brothers René and Pierrot Milelli. From left to right: René Milelli (the eldest), my brother Pierre, Pierrot Milelli (the youngest) and me.

Presentation of the Medal of the Righteous was made on Corsica in Vezzani, near Corte, according to the wishes of the Milelli family, the village where Captain Louis Milelli had lived and is buried and where one of his grandsons lives. For the occasion we had decided, my wife and I that all our family would be present, including my brother who lives in Italy and my youngest son who was then living in London. This ceremony was both a tribute to the memories of Captain Louis Milelli, and of my parents, in whose name Providence allowed me to discharge a debt.

René Marcel Part 2: The Righteous of the Nations-*Unrecognized*, 1943

I want to come back now to our desperate situation at the beginning of 1943. Due to the mortal danger that hung over us, my parents wondered at one point if, to save me, it would not be better to consign me to an underground movement to rescue Jewish children. But Mum could not bring herself to such a separation. To tell you what happened next, I must (as promised) return to Papa's friend René Marcel...

René Marcel, wrongly *not* recognized by Yad Vashem

Papa decided that he should appeal to his friend. Without hesitating for a moment, René Marcel offered to come and join him in Toulouse, because he had a solution to place us in the countryside in a much less dangerous place than Lyon. After leaving part of our furniture in the care of trusted neighbors, we left from the Lyon Perrache railway station by the night train. But each train departure was subject to passenger identity checks. Anticipating this, when the controller knocked on our sleeper compartment, Papa, who had turned off the light, shouted at him: "There is a sick child in here!" The controller didn't insist and walked away. Once again, the danger had receded.

Today, when I happen to return to Lyon, as I move around the city, I find myself in front of places that evoke the tragedy that we lived. I must collect myself when I pass the building at 9, Place des Célestins, the *Palace of Justice*, the notorious *Terminus* hotel where Klaus Barbie and the

School of Military Health sat. I try to re-imagine what our lives were like in this time of terror, lives like flickering flames of candles that the slightest breath could extinguish at any moment.

In Toulouse, René Marcel explained to my father that he bought land for his only son Jacques in Tarn-et-Garonne in the small village of St. Antonin Nobleval. In this way Jacques fell into the category of farmers, which allowed him to escape the terrible *Service du Travail Obligatoire*, or *STO* (in English, the "compulsory labor service"). The *STO* was imposed by Germany on France from 1943. It consisted of sending young French people to Germany to replace German workers who left for the front lines. This is what prompted many of them to join the Resistance, "to go into the bush", as it was then called. On the other hand, other young people joined the Militia. These opposing positions gave rise to a particularly fierce civil war among the French and led to some of the worst excesses.

For the three of us, the problem was different. It was all about getting away from the threat of deportation. At the beginning of 1943 all the French understood that what was happening with the Jews was truly and very serious. Many had already unwittingly witnessed roundups, arrests and above all, the violence that accompanies them. They knew that the Jews thus arrested are herded in various internment camps on French territory, only to be loaded like cattle on freight trains leaving for an unknown destination in the east. Although no one yet suspected that the Jews were doomed to extermination, the sheer brutality with which they are treated upon their arrest unveiled an inhuman tragedy. The news disseminated by leaflets of the Resistance evoked horrible facts. René Marcel understood that in Toulouse, swarming with Germans, collaborators and militiamen, it was too dangerous for us and that we must hide in the countryside. He knew good people in St. Antonin on whose discretion he could count, in particular the family of Raymond and Margot Gracia. Both were a bit younger than Mum and Dad, and they had a baby girl, Colette, two years younger than me. Thanks to René Marcel, we were protected by this family for eighteen months. After the war, my father and the Marcel family also kept in touch. As I write now, I recall a most memorable case of indigestion following an overly generous meal with the Marcel couple who lived in Allée des Soupirs in Toulouse! I saw Marie Marcel again during my military service in 1961 at Toulouse Francazal. By then, she had unfortunately become a widow.

As you will read below, we also kept up our relationship with the Gracia family, one that has continued to this day.

Knowing today all that I have learned about Vichy, I have so many questions that I would have asked René Marcel, who was witness to that terrible time. Now it is too late... I was only twenty-two years old and still totally ignorant of the facts then.

The Stay in St. Antonin Nobleval, April 1943-October 1944

This is how we landed at St. Antonin Nobleval. Dad unfortunately left no written memories of this perilous time in our lives. Writing was not his strong suit. On the other hand, he readily evoked memories of the war. I was already fifty-five years old at Papa's death on January 2, 1995. I had not thought earlier to put these memories in writing by means of methodical research and interviews. Many details of this time are alas, lost. The instinct of self-preservation, the foolish hopes of surviving this ruthless hunt, perhaps even the confidence that the Good God would have mercy on us, nevertheless allowed my parents to find the strength to face the daily grind. More than once, Mum told me that in the months between the arrival of the Germans in Lyon in November 1942 and our departure for Toulouse, she knew a Catholic German, a Madame Hausdorf, originally from Wiesbaden whose husband was Jewish. My parents knew her through another Jew named Gluck, whose wife and son were later deported. Mme. Hausdorf had a clairvoyant talent: she "drew the cards" or spoke of the future with the help of coffee grounds. This was how she predicted that great misfortune would occur to the Dock family of the grocer downstairs. The sad prophesy later proved to be correct when one of Mrs. Dock's children accidentally fell from the balcony and died.

In these times of utter distress and despair that seemed to offer no escape, my parents clung to the slightest sign, however irrational. Mme. Hausdorf used to say to them, "Every time I probe my husband's future, everything is dark. But have no fear, you will be fine." Indeed, her husband *was* deported, and we survived. Mum remembers that Mrs. Hausdorf had a strange, vague look in her eyes, and believed that she may have been had what has come to be called the "gift of double sight. After the war, when I returned to Lyon, my parents were able to see Mme. Hausdorf a few more times. Then, one fine day, she left to join her son in the States, and we never heard from her again. I take pleasure in believing that Providence, having had pity on the despair which tore the hearts of my parents, had sent them a sign which reassured them of a better life. Here then is Mom's own account of our time in St. Antonin.

We arrived in Toulouse at 7 a.m. and René Marcel picked us up at the station. We continued on to St. Antonin with René's son Jacques, where Mr. Raymond Gracia with his daughter Colette on his arm came to welcome us. We spent our first night at St. Antonin with them. Only the Gracia family knew our true identity. To everyone else we were the Wallon family, Walter was Louis Wallon, Maman was Hélène Wallon, née Mayor, and I was called Jacqui Wallon. We spent the next few days in a small hotel and shortly found accommodation on the ground floor of an old house inhabited by Albert Nonorgues, a blind war veteran, who lived on the 1st floor with his maid. The eighteen months that we lived in St. Antonin were relatively happy given the circumstances and remain engraved forever in our memory.

The first weeks were admittedly somewhat ambiguous because the locals regarded us with suspicion; some even suspected us of being agents of the Gestapo. What irony! Shortly after, thanks to Raymond Gracia, Walter met Alex Bugarel, a young man who belonged to a resistance movement and to whom Walter could confide. As Walter appeared regularly in the company of Alex and other young resistance fighters, we ended up being adopted by the village. In any case no one would have taken us for Jews. When we came to spend three weeks' vacation after the war in St. Antonin, a local manufacturer with whom Walter had played bridge from time to time, said: I would have bet half my fortune that you were neither Jewish nor even German. One day M. Gracia reported to us that he had heard certain people say: This Wallon certainly married an Englishwoman (I spoke French with a rather strong English accent) and that is why he settled here. These musings by our neighbors suited us perfectly. But in this place, there were many Jews who had been sent there by the Vichy government. Barely eight days after our arrival the Gestapo came to round them up. There were then heartbreaking scenes where the children were torn from their parents to be loaded into trucks.

You can imagine our state of mind as we helplessly watched these horrific tragedies. The owner of the hotel where we were staying temporarily told us: "Fortunately we don't have Jews in our home!" At noon the Gestapo agents came to lunch precisely in this hotel, sitting just a few meters from our table. We heard from their conversations the names of the Jews they still had to look for and who were hiding in the vineyards. We felt like we were sitting on hot coals when our little Jacqui (3 and a half years old) who still spoke German then said: Why do these people speak German? With a remarkable presence of mind Walter at once feigned anger with the bewildered child: "If you don't want to eat, I'll take you upstairs to the bedroom" and took him out with him! There he explained to him that there was danger in speaking such words. Back with him in the room, he then said to him: "So, you want to eat now?" Fortunately, the Gestapo people hadn't noticed anything wrong with how this scenario played out.

The apartment we moved into had a very large kitchen and an equally large room which served as our living room and bedroom. We had brought Jacqui's little bed as well as our dishes and linen. In short, nothing was missing except a gas stove. So, we had to cook over a fire. This problem was solved very quickly after ordering a stove that was delivered to us soon after, from a hardware store. As regards the provision of food, it was for us who had been really hungry living in Lyon, a real paradise. The ration cards were just a formality, we were able to get as much meat, bread and vegetables as we wanted and thus satiate ourselves. The Gracias were such good people. On the other hand, the young couple Jacques and Francine Marcel (his wife) quarreled regularly: each of them came from a family that had spoiled them, perhaps too much! One day Francine locked her husband all morning in the bathroom, another time all the dishes were thrown in the street. They divorced after the war.

Not wanting to remain idle, Walter he worked with peasants and in various jobs. He quickly forged an excellent reputation as a farm worker, so much so that a peasant offered him a permanent job including the provision of a small house for him and his family. We were convinced that the Allies would land in France by 1943, but the summer passed and nothing of the sort happened. It was then that Walter was hired as a lumberjack by a logging company. The first days of work were very painful for him because his hands were not used to this kind of exercise so that they were bloody at the end of the day. After four or five days he overcame this difficulty and was even happy to be doing this work in open air. He left at 4 a.m., ax on his shoulder, in the direction of the Roc d'Anglars. He arrived after at least an hour walking on mountain paths. He would work until 1 p.m., return around 2 p.m. with a bundle of wood on his back for our fireplace, rest for a good hour, and then go to the cafe to play a game of bridge. Two of his partners were also Jews in hiding under false names. I spent a lot of time alone at home with my little Jacqui and my household. On the advice of neighbors, I enrolled Jacqui in kindergarten. He liked it a lot and this is how he became friends with a little girl named Mado (diminutive of Madeleine), the daughter of Alsatian refugees. Jacqui was easy-to-raise, a child with a very good heart. One day I sent him to buy several apples from an orchard, but he returned with only one apple. When I asked him where the other apples had gone, he replied: "I met some friends from kindergarten and gave them each one. We have one left for us." Yes, he was like that, and everyone liked him.

In the meantime, we managed to get news of Oma Wolf from a trusted person in Lyon and so, we knew that she was in good health. A few old friends visited her every now and then, and she was out of danger anyway. The payment of her monthly rents was made by friends with a wire transfer from a post office which was never the same in order not to arouse suspicion about regular money transfers from St. Antonin. Regarding Papa [my Opa Josef], we never heard from him, though still hoping to find him alive after the war.

Winter came and we found ourselves buried alive in this hole. I read a lot because along one wall was a bookcase. I also sewed and knitted to pass the time. Every so often, the Marcel's visited from Toulouse, which enlivened our apartment. Outside the house, I avoided speaking with people as much as possible. Walter thought there was danger in such contacts because of my poor French. For me, a person with a communicative temperament, it was very hard. Then came Christmas. Toys were very expensive, and the choice was not great. So, I bought a few things to surprise Jacqui. We put everything in a bag which we tied in the chimney flue with a string. In the evening, when it was time to distribute the presents, Walter pulled on the string and the bag fell from the fireplace to Jacqui's amazement. We opened the bag and there was nothing more beautiful or delightful than for us than to see the amazed gaze of a child and to play and to rejoice with him.

One evening during this winter we were invited by friends of the Gracias, the family of Jacques Roussenac, to eat pancakes. We waited until Jacqui had fallen asleep, then we went to these friends' house two houses away and spent about two hours there. It was a very pleasant time. On our way home, we tiptoed into the bedroom to find that the little bed was empty! Distraught, we at once went out into the street to see a neighbor coming towards us with Jacqui in hand. This is how we learned that Jacqui had woken up in the night to realize that we were not there, that he was undoubtedly seized with anguish and ran into the street crying. The brave neighbor, an Alsatian, had taken the child. We were of course grateful and embarrassed when we picked him up. This was a lesson learned because we never left Jacqui alone at home again. The winter seemed very long to us, and one day Jacqui caught a fever accompanied by a rash. He had to stay in bed for a few days. He was already on the road to recovery when to our surprise one fine morning, the kindergarten teacher and the whole class came to visit him. I was very moved by the kindness of this gesture. And one fine evening M. Gracia came by to ask Walter to play violin at a small village festival, which he gladly accepted. But I could not go with him there because we did not want to leave Jacqui alone again. All I know is that Walter came home much pleased. It may seem trivial to recount such trivial facts, but in our monotonous life such events were a welcome, even necessary distraction.

But then there were still other moments, ones of great fear. One Sunday, already in the spring of 1944, we had been invited for coffeecake with the Gracias. I seem to recall that it was on the occasion of a birthday in their family. We were comfortably seated at a table when unexpectedly, someone entered. It turned out he was a gendarme who had come to bring some paper. Because he represented the Vichy regime, he could have been dangerous for us. Mr. Gracia said to him: "Take coffee with us," an invitation he accepted with pleasure. I immediately felt uneasy when he began to ask me indiscreet questions like where I was born in Alsace since he knew the region very well. I gave him very brief answers and, feeling the blush spread over my face, I dropped an object on the ground to pick it up to hide my embarrassment. Immediately my wise Walter picked up the thread of the conversation to change its direction. We were especially worried because this gendarme was suspected of being a collaborator. Walter shared this story and our concern with Alex Bugarel. The latter and his Resistance comrades then stole his bike, leaving a note where to pick it up. He came to the appointed place to find some resolute young men. He was told to be quiet about us and that this would be his first and the last warning. The implied threat had its effect and we never had anything to fear again.

Doctor Paul Marius Bénet and Heroes of the Resistance, 1943

Here I must tell of another event of December 1943, which had left us in "shock and awe". That day Walter went with René Marcel to the station and on the way back, he stopped at the town hall to collect our food ration cards. When he returned, he was as white as chalk. He said: "The police officer handed me a paper that said that I must report to the office." The paper said that there was in St. Antonin a Wallon family from Dunkirk, but for which there was no trace in the Civil Registry. As part of his secret identity, Walter had chosen Dunkirk as his birthplace because the city had been totally destroyed in June 1940 when the British re-embarked. Unfortunately, the authorities had still had the time to transfer the city's archives to Lille. René continued, "I felt such a shock I thought I would pass out. Then, after I calmed down a little, I looked at this paper more closely and saw that it was from the tax authorities. This seemed to me to be more perhaps less threatening and somewhat reasonable. Right away I went to the office and asked the secretary what the meaning of this investigation was". She replied: "It happens sometimes" and asked if I had a family record book and a military record book. "Of course." I replied. Of course, we had excellent false papers and quickly went off to find them. Thereupon the officer made his report and the matter was provisionally settled."

(Author's note: the false papers were preserved, and I can vouch that the military booklet was far from a perfect forgery - I still shudder now.)

But what would have happened to us if the authorities in Toulouse were to continue the search? Mr. Gracia's mother told us that she had gone to school with Doctor Bénet, the mayor of St. Antonin. She said that she knew he would be on our side and would ask him for an appointment. The same evening Walter was invited to meet him. In the doctor's waiting room, he saw a man come out of his house that he thought was Jewish based on his looks and appearance. As soon as he came into the consultation room Walter explained to the Doctor "I am not coming to see you as a doctor but as the mayor. My name is not Wallon but Lévi and I am a Jew!" The doctor first scratched his head worriedly and then said that he had received information that the Gestapo would come in a few days to arrest of Jews. Walter then told him that he was living under a false identity and that in this respect he had nothing to fear. Dr. Bénet asked: "Do you have at least good false papers?" Walter showed his papers to the Doctor. After examining them, Bénet said, "Okay, then everything is in order."

Thereupon Walter showed him the paper from Toulouse. Bénet then expressed the opinion that the tax authorities would be satisfied with the information communicated. "In any case" he added, "if there was a new request, I would see it and go to the office first. In case the situation looked more dangerous, I would have you prepare new false papers right away, and you would disappear from the village." Walter said, "I have had these false papers drawn up for two years and I fully intend to continue." It was only later that we learned that Doctor Bénet had been the leader of the local Resistance! Fortunately, further requests never took place and, once again, we felt that a protective hand had saved us from danger! May the name of Doctor Bénet be blessed even today! He certainly didn't live long since he was an already old man like Grandmother Gracia, and like her, a wonderful person who beamed kindness and was always helpful. And how grateful we were for every word of comfort. In 2011 I went to Taurynia, a Catalan village in the Eastern Pyrenees to pay homage to the grave of Paul Bénet, buried with his wife (née Nicolau from the village), and to pay tribute to his memory.

Before I continue with the rest of our time in St. Antonin, let me return to the day of our arrival in St. Antonin, where Jacques and Francine Marcel first lodged us with them. They quickly drew our attention to a couple who lived in the neighboring house. It was not known where they came from. It was another caution about our potentially dangerous situation. The man's name was Davidson. He looked very Jewish, his wife was a tall blonde Alsatian, and both were suspected of being Gestapo agents. This later proved to be correct. To "protect himself" he had handed over several Jews in hiding to the Gestapo. Every morning I ran into Davidson at the milkman and always felt like he was piercing me with his vulture eyes. Fortunately, he left us in peace, but anguish and terror gripped you as soon as you saw him from afar, a reminder to be careful and that we were not truly safe, not even in St. Antonin. I note here that at the war's end, Davidson was caught by the people of the Resistance who "ironed" his feet flat with irons. It was then that he confessed everything and was sentenced by a regular court to several years in prison. When years later we passed him in Lyon, we of course deliberately ignored him.

Our Transition from St. Antonin Nobleval to Lyon, 1943

I was not four when we arrived and I was five when we left for Lyon, having stayed in St. Antonin for about eighteen months. So, my memories of this stay are virtually nonexistent and boil down to a few incidents that become important to a child; remember that most of what I know is from the recollections of Maman, and not my own. One memory is of a fall from a bicycle luggage rack, where Emile, a boy three or four years older than me, had put me. I had been more afraid than hurting from a few nettle burns. Emile was undoubtedly a rather simple boy; children my age used to hail him mockingly in rhyme: "Emile – imbecile". Another vivid memory comes from one of our excursions to Murel, a village near St. Antonin. Jacques Marcel (René Marcel's son), about ten years younger than Papa, had settled there. During that visit he had perched me on the branch of a tree, from which I couldn't get down without help. He was laughing to see me enraged, weeping and screaming all the swear words I'd had time to learn at my age. Jacques had just married Francine a few months earlier in October 1942 and Mum already related, this unfortunate household led a stormy life that ended in divorce in 1946. Their only daughter, Jacqueline, born in

1944 in Toulouse, was first raised by her grandparents, then by Francine. Jacques remarried twice and died still young (around 70 years old) a few years ago. He had never looked after his daughter or tried to see her again. It was in November 1961, when at the age of twenty-two I had come to study for my military service at the Toulouse-Francazal air base, I saw Francine and Jacqueline, in the meantime renamed Sophie by her mother. There is a bit more to this story, but let us not anticipate...

I also remember a few songs I learned during our stay in St. Antonin. One was a traditional nursery rhyme called *Il Était Un Petit Navire* (*It Was a Small Ship*), and the other for adults, sentimental and nostalgic, entitled *La Rue de Notre Amour* (*The Street of Our Love*). I sang the first song to my own sons many times when they were little, as I do to my grandsons again. The second, *The Street of Our Love*, is doubly nostalgic because it has remained in my memory closely linked to our eighteen months in St-Antonin, and also because it is linked to an amusing anecdote. This now-forgotten period song was premiered in 1940 and was performed by a popular singer Damia, also forgotten. My parents, encouraged by news of Allied victories over the retreating Germans on all fronts, rediscovered moments of youth and recklessness and a re-birth of hope of survival. At these moments they found the desire to sing. *La Rue de Notre Amour* was in full vogue and came regularly to their lips. I heard the well-known singer Damia (and my parents) sing this popular song so often that I learned it myself and sang it, though with a southwest French accent. I was just five years old. You too can now sing along to both songs at:

Il était un petit navire  and

La Rue De Notre Amour

It seems to me that just a few months later, back in liberated Lyon, my parents planted me in the middle of a room in a coffee house at the corner of avenue de Saxe and rue Bugeaud. The boss of the café was Mme. Devaux. Duly informed of my skill, she asked me to sing the famous song in front of the seated consumers. And I, without any fear or stage fright, began to sing, among other things, the following verse, which with my southwestern accent, managed to provoke the general hilarity of all present:

"It is the street of our love, at the bottom of an old suburb, we see there prowling in the evening, lovers in black corners. It is the street of our desires, where love has flourished. At the bottom of an old suburb, it is the lane of faithful hearts. We still love always, the street of our love".

In St. Antonin we rented rooms at 7, rue de la Pélisserie. Recall that the blind Mr. Albert Nonorgues lived on the ground floor. Although our false identity papers testified that we were "real" French, my parents' foreign accents could easily have led our landlord to doubt our 'Frenchness', and to conclude that we were in reality Jewish refugees under a false identity. If he did surmise this, then he must also have known that if the Germans discovered us, it would have serious consequences for him and his family at a time when the Germans strictly prohibited any "authentic" French citizen from concealing Jews by housing them (knowingly or not, with or without financial compensation).

What makes me think that Albert Nonorgues had guessed our condition as refugees comes from a lie he told to the German SS. This is according to the verbal account given several times by my father, the essence of which follows:

Following the Anglo-American landing on June 6, 1944, all German units scattered around France were called to join the Normandy military front, including a detachment from the "das Reich" Division stationed at St. Antonin. Before leaving the village, the soldiers attacked the inhabitants both to loot them and to flush out any resistance fighters. Thus, one evening some of them forced the entrance to Albert Nonorgues' apartment and, following him, were about to open the door to the room where my parents and I lived. Nonorgues, perhaps fearing that the revelation of a couple foreigners not among his relations would pose serious problems for him, took upon himself the serious risk of lying to declare to them in a peremptory tone: "Here, this is the cellar!". It was a moment when, in my opinion, and according to common sense, our life as well as that of Nonorgues was played out with a poker bluff. In the end, miraculously, the soldiers did not insist on entry ("to the cellar") and, thanks to our landlord's courageous lie, our mortal fate was averted.

I have reflected many times on this crucial episode of our stay in the village in June 1944 and I am now convinced that Albert Nonorgues, by diverting (by his lie) the eruption of the German soldiers into my parents' room, saved our lives.

Most of our stay was brought to my attention by my father's stories, but it was not enough for me. Over the years, I have come to realize the true measure of the horrific fate that we were given to escape. It was in 1956, I think, at the age of seventeen that I saw for the first time on television the documentary film directed by Alain Resnais, *Nuit et Brouillard* (*Night and Fog*) about the horror of the Nazi concentration camps. That evening, shortly before the screening, I came to wish my parents goodnight as usual, telling them: "It's nothing for me, moreover, I have to get up early tomorrow. to go to school. "-" Jacki," replied my father, for once, I ask you to stay because I consider it necessary that you know what we escaped." What we did not know at the time was that French censors had cut sequences where the cap of a French gendarme appeared in the film. Since the war ended, de Gaulle was creating the myth of a resistant France, obscuring and erasing anything that could recall French collaboration in abetting the Jewish genocide and in the genocide itself. Apparently, de Gaulle could admit that here and there among the French, there were a few black sheep, but that this was the exception, and that post-war generations had to be made to believe that only the Germans bore the responsibility for the Shoah. The censorship of this film is just one of many examples of the cover-up of French complicity in the genocidal enterprise of exterminating the Jewish people. Other films, books and stories by survivors have since added to this information. Over the years, I learned that all of Europe was jointly responsible, to varying degrees, for the Shoah. It hasn't been said enough, yet it is good that the world knows this, to know and to never forget. I also know that only two nations of Europe, Denmark and Bulgaria, rescued most their Jews from deportation by the Nazis. In Denmark (nominally a German ally at the start of the war), government ministers and resistance fighters arranged for the secret evacuation of Jews to Sweden just hours before the deportations were to begin. In Bulgaria (in fact a German ally), actions of courageous Bulgarian prelates and parliamentarians happened just in time to block imminent deportations. This too the world should never forget.

I have no memory of ever having suffered hunger. On the other hand, Papa always spoke of the hunger in Lyon that had constantly gripped them, Mum and him. Occupied France lacked the most basic foodstuffs such as potatoes, rice, and other vegetables. We ate Jerusalem artichokes or rutabagas, normally reserved for pigs and which typically caused colic in those who ate them. It is in my parents' memory of those difficult times that I was raised to respect food. I was forbidden to be difficult in front of a dish that I didn't want to taste. As a child, I didn't like boiled potatoes or carrots. Yet I had to swallow them under threat of punishment. After the war, butter was a luxury, and it was a long time before we could afford to buy it.

It would never have occurred to me to leave food on my plate. Even today, I feel indignant, or at least very annoyed when I see sated guests leave abundant food on the table, food that their parents would have thrown out without a second thought.

The Gracia Family, also 1943-1944

I could not write my memoirs without a special chapter devoted to the Gracia family who played a vital role in the life of my parents and mine to this day. Once again, it is to our rescuer René Marcel that we owe our contact with this family when we arrived in St. Antonin Nobleval, a village in Tarn-et-Garonne in April 1943, in the heart of the turmoil that almost swallowed us up.

St. Antonin Nobleval is one of the oldest medieval towns at the confluence of the Bonnette and Aveyron rivers. Tourists take pleasure in wandering at random in very old alleys dating back several centuries. You have already read how my mother remembers that when we arrived in St. Antonin with Jacques Marcel (René's son), we were warmly welcomed by Raymond who was carrying his two-year-old daughter Colette in his arms.

During our entire stay in the village, Raymond and his wife Marguerite (Margot) were the only ones who knew us under our true identity and were a constant source of moral support for my parents. Raymond was the very embodiment of kindness. Margot, an energetic and quick-witted woman, was a specialist in the *langue d'oc* (the French spoken southern province of Languedoc). Later, after the war, on each of our visits, she and I established a close bond and we had endless conversations in which I shared with her my experiences as a student. Raymond listened to us willingly and let his wife do much of the talking; she was obviously the pillar of the family. I'm sure Raymond would have been more than willing to enjoy a one-to-one conversation with me, but the opportunity didn't present itself!

I will never forget that when, after Dad received the disturbing questionnaire from the prefecture of Tarn-et-Garonne, it was thanks to Raymond's mother that my father was able to meet the mayor of the village, Dr. Paul Bénet. I remind the reader that Bénet was affiliated with the Resistance, already taking great risks to ensuring the flight of many Jewish refugees in the village when they were being claimed by the Prefecture. So, he was able to reassure my father about the possibilities available to us, should administrative inquiries threatening our security proceed further than the letter.

For all these reasons, Mayor, Dr. Paul Marius Bénet deserves the title of Righteous of Nations a thousand times over, but alas, no one was found to sponsor him to the Yad Vashem Institute.

Once peace returned my parents, my brother and I returned to St. Antonin on several occasions, notably to attend

Colette's first communion in 1954. I was fifteen years old. I remember that after the meal, Colette and her friend Annie Serdot sang in duet a charming, then fashionable song creted by tenor Luis Mariano, the "Nightingale of My Loves". Once again, you can listen to this song at

Luis Mariano-Nightingale of My Loves:

In 1962 (at the age of twenty-three), while I was doing my military service at the Francazal air base, near Toulouse, the entire Gracia family including the parents, Colette, her brother Claude, and her sister Hélène, (the latter two born after the war) came to visit me. I was moved to see the strength of the family's attachment to Colette's fond memories. I am happy to report that Colette eventually married Bernard, a boy with a gift for initiative and for entrepreneurship. Bernard set up a factory making canned duck liver. His business prospered, ensuring Colette a good life. This is how they were able to buy and furnish with exquisite taste, a superb house located in La Capelle Balaguier, a hamlet of 300 inhabitants.

Much later, in 1970, I spent a few months alone in Pau as part of a mission on behalf of the Israeli subsidiary of the helicopter engine manufacturer Turboméca. I had a company car that I could use on weekends. When I realized that the distance from Pau to St. Antonin was less than 300 km, I decided that a weekend trip was quite possible. Leaving very early on Saturday morning I arrived at around 11 a.m. on the main square of St. Antonin. There, I called out to a passer-by who obviously lived in the village because of his worker's garments. "Hello Sir, could you direct me to where Raymond Gracia lives? "Raymond Gracia? But it's very easy. I just saw him with his truck delivering drinks to the cafe 100 yards from here. You will certainly find him in the cellar." So, I went down to the cellar of the cafe in question and found Raymond busy arranging the boxes he had just delivered. Seeing me in the dim light and a hundred leagues from knowing who I was, he said: "Hello sir, can I help you with something?" I burst out laughing and said, "OK then Raymond, do you not recognize me?" He stared at me intently, and then suddenly exclaimed: "Well then, Jacqui, what a pleasant surprise! Oh, how glad I am to see you." And we embraced each other with much emotion. Over and over he repeated: "If I could have imagined for a moment that I would see you today!" Then, leaving his cases where they were, he said: "Get in the truck. We are going to surprise Margot". When we got home, we found Margot on the doorstep who, at once upon seeing me, exclaimed: "Jacqui! (Shaki) from Lyon" (imitating my mother's German accent), "Come here and let me give you a kiss!" And that is how I came to spend a most wonderful weekend with Raymond and Margot, recalling many, many memories of the years '43 and '44.

They took me on a tour of the village, a real pilgrimage where every alley, almost every house was linked to inhabitants who had known us under our pseudonyms, Louis, Hélène and Jacqui Wallon. Those hours we spent Saturday and Sunday, immersed in remembrances, were moments of true happiness in my life. With them I had found my past as a hidden child, as a hidden Jew along with my parents.

On another occasion, passing through Toulouse for my work a few days before Christmas in 1993, I phoned Colette to say hello. She then said to me: "What, you are so close to us! But come spend Christmas with my parents and my family." The offer could not have been more tempting, and after explaining over the phone to my wife in Paris the extraordinary importance of the opportunity of this visit, I could accept wholeheartedly. I was fifty-four at the time, Margot and Raymond, still in good health, were around eighty years old. Now I feel it deeply when, twenty-three years later, I remember the Christmas Eve that I spent with Colette and Bernard and the entire Gracia family at La Capelle Balaguier. It was the purest of luck that we could celebrate in Colette and Bernard's beautiful home, the 50th anniversary of our arrival in St. Antonin and the miraculous survival of our family through the heart of period so tragic to so many others. What a joy it was to see them again! Tears come to my eyes just writing about this historic Christmas.

Since the passing of my parents and Colette's parents, and still moved by the memory of Vichy, I return at regular intervals to collect myself in St. Antonin and to find Colette and her family to whom I feel so closely linked, as to a genuine family. In the meantime, Nathalie, Colette's only daughter is now the mother of three charming little boys who contribute to the happiness of Colette, who was now a widow, as I became a widower in 2017. There is a bond and an understanding between Colette and me that make her the sister I never had. The current that passes between us is invaluable. May we enjoy it, in as good health as possible, for a long time to come!

The Return to Lyon, 1944

For some 240,000 surviving Jews of France, including my parents, the Liberation meant a return to life, an end to a long and dreadful nightmare, an emergence from hiding, the chance finally, to breathe freely. No more the angst that comes from the constant fear of being caught, the terror of separation, or the prospect of a horrific end.

Nearly 80,000 Jews, including 11,000 children, had been caught in the web of the Franco-Nazi predators, interned and ultimately deported to their deaths. As soon as Papa learned of the Allied liberation of Lyon on September 3, 1944 (less than three months after the D-Day landings in Normandy), he decided to go to Lyon to scout possible lodgings and the possibility of resuming his work as a sales representative. That done, he returned to St. Antonin to pick us up. Our departure was surely the moment for a joyful but bittersweet farewell to the few families, the Gracias and their friends, those who had freely given us their moral support, comfort, and affection.

We must have arrived in Lyon in October, at which time we moved into a small 2-room apartment on the top (5th) floor of a building located in the 6th arrondissement at 69 rue Bugeaud at the corner of rue Garibaldi. My parents called this top-floor apartment under the roof of the building a "dovecote", as if it were a home fit for only for us and pigeons! All the windows of our apartment faced the windows of the apartment in front of ours where there lived a young woman of about thirty-five years. She could have been better looking but she was quite tall and strongly built with a broad face, energetic demeanor, and intelligent gaze. Her name of Simone Garnier. She came from a good family of industrialists who owned the *Annonay* paper mill in Ardèche. She was also fluent in English, having been raised by an English governess. She and mum quickly became friends and confidantes, in no small part because Mum appreciated her open-mindedness and the chance to speak English together. At the very bottom of the building, there was an inner courtyard without any ornamental plants to dispel a sadness that it seemed to inspire. On the fourth floor lived a lovely couple, the Tardys, who had taken a liking to me. I also remember other couples, the Laudier, the Bouquet, the Lyonnais and a very beautiful young woman with many admirers, a Mlle. Arlaud. On the ground floor, as one would exit the corridor leading to the stairwell, a door on the right opened onto into the pharmacy dispensary of Miss Marie-Louise Mollard, a tall woman with an unforgiving physique and a masculine sounding voice. Although single, she was the mother of a little girl, Marie-France, who was a bit younger than me. The door to the left in the same corridor opened into the Café Roland. Nothing remains of this building, the pharmacy, or the café - modern construction has erased all of my childhood past, leaving me only with fond memories of sites and neighbors.

Another such memory; there was also on ground floor, a poor, worn-out old woman who was all the uglier with age because she had only one prominent tooth left on her upper jaw. Her name was Madame Bansac and hers was a very small apartment which opened onto the courtyard. Subconsciously cruel, I used to mimic her toothless mouth in front of my parents, who laughed and scolded me gently. I also sometimes made her go crazy by throwing a "water bomb" out of our apartment window made from a cleverly folded sheet of paper that I filled with water. Shards of paper then spread at the bottom of the courtyard, which had the effect of raising Mme. Bansac to a black fury. Since I was the only kid in the building who lived on the courtyard side, she knew that the culprit could only be me, so I found myself punished by Mum (Dad was either at work or at the bistro where he played bridge) whenever I indulged in this kind of mischief.

I didn't have much affection for Simone, who I found to be too much of an authoritarian. Also, she would monopolize Mom's attention whenever we went out with her, with the result that I didn't have anyone to talk to during the walk. When I say "we", it was always Mom, Simone and me. Dad worked, it is true, or played bridge, but even if he was free, he did not admit the presence of a third party in the family, especially a neighbor if she was a woman. His relations with Simone were limited to those of strict courtesy. As for me, I have a precise and bitter memory of a walk I took alone with Simone in the Parc de la Tête d´Or on a freezing winter morning. It was so cold that that my hands, even with gloves on, ached so terribly that I begged Simone to rush me home. She, who must have received the benefits of a Spartan education, clearly intended to share them with me. She was completely indifferent to my pleas, which quickly turned into tears; she stubbornly refused to cut short the walk. When I got home, I complained bitterly to Mom, so much so that I never went on a one-on-one walk with her again.

Mom very much enjoyed speaking English with Simone. This gave them the luxury in a France whose inhabitants at that time knew little or nothing about foreign languages, of being able to express themselves freely in the street without running the risk of an unwanted or untimely intrusion of a third party into their conversation. One time while walking in the park, this certainty of privacy, of being "unheard" by the public played a bad trick on them. At the bend of an alley, Simone saw a man sitting on a bench reading his newspaper. Noticing that he was hunchbacked, Simone, still speaking aloud, said to Mom, "Oh, regarde ce petit bossu!" (Oh, look at that little hunchback!). As they walked past him, the man continued unperturbed to read his newspaper. To Simone's suddenly sheepish embarrassment, she realized he was reading *The London Times*!

Long after having long passed the age of 25, Simone, wearing the 'cap of Saint Catherine', remained an old maid. She had lovers though, who must have given her the legitimate physical satisfactions she sought, but who were intellectually inferior to her. Therefore, her connections to these men were, not surprisingly, quite brief.

She would talk about them to Mom sarcastically, giving them all kinds of nicknames. One of them, who had lasted a little longer than the others, she baptized with the sobriquet "the beanpole" (a tall, poorly built, gangly-looking man). By dint of hearing her talk to Mum about her "beanpole", I was convinced that that was his real name. So that one day when the couple came to our house for a visit, Mum asked me to tell him: "Hello Sir" to show that I was a well-behaved child. Wanting to be zealous, I proudly exclaimed, to show that I had identified him correctly, "Hello Mr. Escogriffe!" Mom and Simone were seized with giggles; I guess they were a little embarrassed. Considering the level of education of Simone's boyfriend, he must have been surprised without understanding the meaning of his nickname, which is not widely used in everyday conversation.

Poor Simone! She ended up attached to a married man, arguably a man unhappy in his own household, and much older than she was. He adored Simone in whom he found, if not beauty, at least youth, liveliness and undeniable originality. Oddly enough, his name was Simonin. Either inadvertently or as she wished, she found herself pregnant by him and eventually gave birth to a baby girl. Pregnancies are not without danger, and if anything, even more so then. Simone, who despite her sturdy demeanor was in poor health, did not survive her delivery. Her baby was taken care of by Simone's family as well as by her natural father. Sadly, with Simone's death Mom lost probably the only great French friend she had in her life.

Simone had also spent time with Marie-Louise Mollard, the pharmacist on the ground floor, who, in addition her strong intellect had the courage to freely assume the role of single mother, something frowned on at the time. Simone's death brought Maman closer to Marie-Louise, so much so that even after we moved in October 1949, they continued to see each other for years. And this is how and why I befriended her daughter Marie-France, a little younger than me. I saw her at regular but rather spaced intervals. She was a cheerful, funny girl and I enjoyed talking to her. After she married, I lost touch with her.

Our apartment in rue Bugeaud belonged to a Monsieur Olagnon. It consisted of a living room with an alcove where my parents slept, a small adjacent kitchen and my bedroom ventilated by a skylight, i.e., an oblique skylight that one opened upwards by pushing on a steel rod. Our toilets did not flush. We therefore used a container "pitcher", which as I can still remember, had a so-called swan's beak shape. The pitcher had to be filled with water and then emptied into the bowl after each use. In short, a perfect comfort!

Winters in Lyon could be very cold, against which we used a coal stove to heat ourselves. There were two grades of this coal: *coke*, which is cheaper but less caloric, and the higher energy *anthracite*. Papa, while we were in hiding, had used up his savings and had to make do with coke. We bought the coal at the start of the winter and stored it in the cellar. Regularly, Papa had to go down the five floors, then to the cellar and then to climb back up all the way with the bucket full of coal. Of course, summer in Lyon is hot and stuffy. Living under the roof, we felt it even more, especially Papa, who was very sensitive to the heat. At that time, we did not yet know the benefits of a refrigerator (let alone an air conditioner!). We used an "icebox", a small piece of furniture in which we put a block of ice bought from a traveling iceman who sold these blocks on the platform of a cart pulled by a wretched nag. Even so it was difficult to keep the butter which could quickly go rancid. Since our windows were open for a little fresh, if not always cool air, the sound of neighboring radios reached us easily and we could hear the popular singers of the day, like Edith Piaf singing her famous *La vie en rose*. Listen to this song at:

La Vie en Rose

Dad had resumed his job as a sales representative in leather goods, a luxury sector. If life had been easy before the war, the same could not be said for a country ravaged by five years of occupation which now lacked everything, including food. For almost two years after the Liberation, the French were rationed with a ticket system. It was therefore more lucrative to market butter, eggs and cheese than handbags for ladies. But Dad preferred to continue in a field that he knew well. He was the multi-card representative of several enterprises, including that of Jean Rendu, a Lyon leather goods manufacturer. M. Rendu had difficulty fulfilling orders taken by Papa due to the shortage of raw materials needed to make the bags. Dad also represented a firm owned by Jules Holtz that manufactured ladies' compacts. The commissions came in irregularly, bringing an income which allowed us to live without ever lacking the bare necessities, but otherwise sparely. Dad didn't want Mum to work, so that we were completely dependent on him.

Sometimes there was not enough money for clothing. I was probably growing too fast for Dad's taste because every request from Mum for money to buy me new shoes annoyed him. Sometimes Mum would take advantage of him while he was asleep to extract a few bills from Daddy's wallet. Despite this materially narrow life, the five years spent in rue Bugeaud - November 1944 to November 1949 - remained in my parents' memory the happiest years of their post-war existence because they could relish the flavor of rediscovered freedom. The spirit of economy that reigned in our little family had such a profound impact on my life, reflected in a thousand little disadvantages. My sons, who grew up well off, had difficulty understanding such details. One detail: often, on summer walks with Mum in the Tête d'Or Park, I would ask her to buy me an ice cream or other sweets that I loved. The refusals with which she opposed me because of her meager budget deeply frustrated the child that I was. Even today, when I come back to Lyon and go for a walk in this suburban park where I have so many childhood memories, I buy for the child that I was the treat, now so commonplace, of which I was then deprived. In the years 1945-47 when everything was rationed (especially meat), chicken, which nowadays is a common commodity, was considered a great luxury that we could not afford. I remember a visit we paid on a winter Sunday to friends of my parents, the Finkelsteins. Their only son, Raymond, a year older than me, was a loud-mouth and thought he knew everything better than everyone else. His father was a tailor, and His mother was short and plump, with a heavy male voice. I can still see her, busy in her kitchen, opening her oven a crack to see a superb roasting chicken already golden brown. I was fascinated by this spectacle, appetizing both for sight and aroma.

Of course, when I got home, I asked sourly "why don't we ever eat chicken at home?" I think I remember that the anger that seized my parents, who did not want to discuss this topic, made me regret asking the question.

The Municipal School at 25 Rue Pierre Corneille; Life in Lyon, 1944-1949

When we returned to Lyon at the end of 1944, my parents enrolled me in a nursery school on rue de Créqui, a few meters from rue Bugeaud. My mistress (with all due honor), Mlle. (Miss) Vernet, took an affection for me, perhaps after learning by what a miracle we had escaped annihilation. She also admired how easily I learned to read the alphabet, then words, then sentences. Therefore, twice-pampered, I was happy in this kindergarten and gladly returned to Mlle. Vernet the tenderness with which she showered me. I learned to read very quickly, ahead of most of my little comrades. I still remember my first book which was *Les Vacances de Mamichou* (*Mommys Holidays*). As for its content, I forgot it a long time ago. In the same year, I believe I managed to decipher *Pinocchio*, Carlo Collodi's masterpiece. Perhaps with the encouragement of Mlle. Vernet, my parents lulled themselves into an illusion that their offspring was gifted. So, when it came to enrolling me in the municipal school at 25 rue Pierre Corneille, the Director, Mr. Colomb, a jovial man of strong build, duly impressed by the ease with which I read him a passage from a book chosen at random, immediately agreed to let me skip the 1st class, the "Elementary course 1st year". As of this writing, my municipal school building still exists. Walking briskly, it takes a little less than half an hour to get there from our home on rue Bugeaud. Just walk in the direction of the Rhône. After crossing place St. Pothin and Avenue de Saxe, turn right into the first street, rue Pierre Corneille. About 50 meters further stands a dark, stern-looking building with two separate entrances, one inscribed "Girls" and the other for "Boys". It was there, on October 1, 1945, that, only six years old, I left what had been for me a kindergarten paradise thanks to Miss Vernet, to enter the 2nd year preparatory course, officiated by Mme. Dimet. She was kind of a dry woman, without age, who professed no particular sympathy towards me. Also, if I was nominally at the same level as my classmates in reading, I was missing a year in the other disciplines, especially in arithmetic. The consequences were not long in coming; from the first term, I found myself at the bottom of the class. My mother in some distress came to consult Mme. Dimet to try to understand the reasons for this situation, which my parents considered shameful. Mme. Dimet threw her arms to the sky, saying with a disgusted air: "Your son, dear madam, he's a slack, a slacker!" So, back home, I was roundly lectured by Mum and Dad that it was the end of the good life in kindergarten, that at my age Dad was always first, that I had to listen to what was being said in class, not to day-dream and that I must start taking life more seriously and above all, I must not *take it easy*. Papa then took it into his head to make me understand, with lots of examples, the rudiments of calculation which seemed an insurmountable logic to me. "You understood?" he asked me. "Yes, Dad." I replied, as much to please him as to have peace. Asked to perform an exercise based on the examples given but which I did not understand at all, I remained silent and embarrassed. Dad would repeat the examples in a tone that announced the coming storm. Seeing that he was hitting a concrete wall of incomprehension, he got angry. Desperate, I burst into tears, which ended the private lesson along with my torment, for me a bitter escape.

At such times my mother, in pity, would put me to bed saying to me: "Come on, Jacqui, tomorrow it will be better". However, it did not get better at all. I was all the less motivated as Ms. Dimet, who was by no means a teacher, was deeply unpleasant to me. My ranking did not improve much throughout the year, but at least I managed not to have to repeat a grade; this would have been the height of shame and dishonor for my parents.

The school schedule was quite demanding for such young children: from 8 a.m. to noon and from 2 p.m. to 5 p.m. Monday to Saturday, with only Thursday afternoons and Sundays free. And when we got home, we still had to do the homework and learn the recitations (short speeches to be given in class). This is when and how, at six years of age, I got acquainted to my great displeasure with the works of La Fontaine. Indeed, the 17th century language of La Fontaine was incomprehensible. For example, I had to memorize *Le petit poisson et le pêcheur* (*The little fish and the fisherman*). In this fable are lines of such abstract and difficult grammatical structure as *Un tiens vaut, ce dit-on, mieux que deux tu l'auras* (Yours is worth, they say, better than the two you will have...), the comprehension of which was inaccessible to me. The line amounted to memorizing and reciting a succession of meaningless sounds. I doubt that Mme. Dimet was ever able to bring the children that we were to any understanding of a line of this difficulty. Noting that La Fontaine composed this fable 300 years earlier, in the language of his time, one could be forgiven for questioning the mental health of the national education system that allowed (or required) teachers to present such reading assignments. Since my parents had not studied in France, they could never have helped me in this area. From this point of view, I was at a disadvantage compared to my French parent comrades. Nevertheless, I learned this fable as one would swallow cod liver oil, without realizing that years later I would have such pleasure reciting it, and by heart to boot!

At the time, the educational system was largely based on memorization and not on reflection. The chapters of history, geography, French or "lessons in things" (that is, natural sciences) were always ended with a summary in bold characters and in a frame that we had to learn by heart and recite on the blackboard at the request of the master. In this way, like my comrades, I learned (I Jacques Lévi, a distant descendant of the patriarch Jacob of the Bible) that "our ancestors were the Gauls". Although I was born into the Jewish faith, I was also born French. Thus, attending a

French school, it was above all, important to the Republic (as to my parents for that matter), that my education made me a good child, to be and speak average French and, if possible, to be above average. Mom and Dad had told me on several occasions that we were of the Jewish religion, though I think that we were more inclined to say Israelite, a term considered at the time less indecent and more acceptable. But, apart from the fact that being an Israelite demarcated a line between us and other French citizens, I didn't understand at all what that difference was, nor its significance, at least not during my schooling in the primary classes. As you will read, trouble started for me only after high school, albeit in a moderate way.

Returning briefly to learning by rote, on further reflection the system had at least some utility, including multiplication tables, French grammar rules, and what we call *civics* today, and the French departments (regions) and their capitals that have been engraved on me for life.

On a visit to Lyon in May 2004 to celebrate Mum's 90th birthday, I found most of my old class photos. In the one from the 1945-46 class (below), Mrs. Dimet, is missing, but Mr. Colomb, the manager (the "dirlo" as he was called) is standing at the left.

Elementary class 2nd year 1945-46; I am seated in front 3rd from the right

As I contemplate the faces of my comrades, some names come back to me: Martin, the gifted blond (top right, who was later to contract meningitis); Marc; Forestier; Roux (last on the right in the middle row, still scared, fearing to receive some blow); Tissot (middle row, 3rd from the right, always with the worried air of an adult); Roussel (middle row, 6th from the left in a black coat, not very smart - he had stolen the money from the canteen; but after investigation by the manager, he did confess and returned the money); Briday (sitting to my right in a black shirt with stories to make your hair stand on end - one day he assured me with the utmost seriousness that when I got home I would find my mother dead, for which I had never forgiven him - but who would carry my schoolbag when we went out while I would walk behind him reading a book. For some reason, my parents nicknamed him the "mashoress" (*servant* in Yiddish). Praire (bottom row, 4th from left) looked like a girl). Finally, Mayen (1st from left in front), an awful prankster who once, during a dictation when Mme. Dimet announced, "open the quotes", slipped into my ear "open Mme. Dimet's panties". I broke out in a fit of uncontrolled laughter, after which Mme. Dimet made me copy fifty times the injunction: "you don't laugh during class")!

At this time, television did not yet exist and radio had a strong hold on family lives. Voices and music floated between neighbors from window to window. What I remember most are songs, especially those sung by Edith Piaf, André Dassary, Tino Rossi, Maurice Chevalier, Berthe Sylva and others. One, dating back to 1926, was Berthe Sylva's often broadcast rendition of *Les Roses Blanches* (*The White Roses*), about a child and his poor, dying mother. When I heard this song for the first time, I was seven years old. Upset by the lyrics I burst into tears and ran into Maman's arms. Understanding the reason for my grief, she consoled me, saying "Don't cry any more since you..., you have your Maman". Hear the song as I did at:

Berthe Sylva - The White Roses
In our neighborhood the petty bourgeois rubbed shoulders with people of more modest means and all the children knew each other. We loved to play in the street, which very

much distressed Mum. There were the Mons brothers, whose father was a tailor at home and who corrected his children with a "swift", a whip with several straps that kept on a nail on the wall. Then there was Roger. He lived in an apartment with a toilet in a wooden cubicle on the balcony. Acting as if he was sitting in this WC, he boasted crudely of his scatological prowess; eventually I stopped visiting him. Rémy was my courtyard playmate. He lived on the ground floor and took satisfaction at every opportunity to slander his adult sister. Mum suffered a lot from these associations which supplied me a lexicon of swear-words to go with insolent reflections..., all of which earned me reprimand and severe punishment. In German, Maman called these families *Koress Leute*, meaning people of nothing.

During the torrid summers of Lyon, among the street noises that I recall are the cries of itinerant craftsmen such as "viiii-itrier" (a glazier), of the grinder (who sharpened knives), or the "iceman" carrying blocks of ice in his cart pulled by an old nag. I can still see the iceman with his jute apron cutting small blocks at the peak for the happy owners of a "cooler". The latter was the ice box, a small thermally insulated cupboard holding blocks of ice. This was long before the wide availability of real refrigerators and as I mentioned earlier, our makeshift installations would barely stop butter from melting and going rancid.

I was happy in this time so soon after the war, but for two quite different reasons. One was the intense relief my parents felt to breathe freely after the years of Occupation had to rub off on me and lift my spirits. The other (maybe this is even the same) reason was that most of the other people I knew emanated a genuine joy of living. I remember in particular the Bastille Day feast on July 14 which in 1945 was accompanied by popular balls in the streets of my neighborhood. In addition, it often happened at these impromptu parties, that accordionists gathered at folding tables at a crossroads; surrounded by a crowd of onlookers (including me), performed popular songs of the day. Those present would sing together and bought or sold scores of these songs. One of these songs, repeated by the radio and by the children, completely forgotten since, was called *Ploum ploum tra-la-la*, which you can listen to at:

Un Zany-Ploum ploum tra-la-la

Zany, all the rage at the time, was an art of saying or singing whatever comes to mind, even if it doesn't make a lot of sense. After years of anguish, fear and mistrust the time had finally come to let off steam, to let go, in short, to feel free.

In the summer of 1945, my father decided to go to the United States to see his family, his parents, his brothers, sisters, nephews and nieces in Chicago. I guess everyone had contributed to pay for this trip across the Atlantic Ocean. There were two reasons for this decision: one was just the joy of seeing his loved ones again after such a hard separation during which our life had hung by only a thread. The other was that his older brother Robert's days were numbered due to an incurable arthritis whose effects had already led to the amputation of both his legs, with more amputations pending. While he was visiting, I guess the family had tried to convince Papa to join them in the US where they thought it would have been easier for him to build a more comfortable material existence. At the end of a stay of some six weeks, Papa came to the conclusion that the price of this comfort would be too high for him. I found a machine-dictated letter from him describing the family's invitation, (now kept among my personal documents). The different climate, the family's promiscuity which very quickly became unbearable, and the frantic, obsessive hunt for the dollar made the invitation quite unattractive. France's more temperate climate, a certain relaxed rhythm of life even if rationing was still in effect, and the good-natured mentality of the average Frenchman who does not take life too seriously, were more important to him. "I might have made more money, but I would have lived ten years less," he told me.

What little I learned about the USA during a similar stay 15 years later led me to the same conclusion.

Mum and I went up to Paris in September to welcome Papa on his return. We stayed with Aunt Yvonne and Uncle Maurice Steinberg (whom I have already mentioned above) at their home on the rue Lécluse in the 17th arrondissement, near the Clichy metro station. The only memory I have of this, my first contact with Paris, is the characteristic smell of the metro. Maurice was a jeweler and worked nearby. Their son Robert, a doctor, had married Jeannette, a Protestant nurse of Polish origin that he had met during the war. A daughter was born from this union, Françoise, followed by Jean-Michel who was still an infant. They had taken up residence in Colombes, in the Paris suburbs where they remained all their lives. Mum must have seemed very provincial to Aunt Yvonne, so attached as she was to her status as an experienced Parisian. She directed each of our steps with so much authority that I wanted to say to Mum: "My word, it looks like she commands all of Paris!" But..., I did not! Their other son Armand, the eldest, had returned from deportation. A doctor, too, he had married a former divorced dancer (also not Jewish, and the mother of a little girl). Even though Armand had by some miracle, survived Auschwitz, Aunt Yvonne and Uncle Maurice disapproved of this union, resulting in enmity and ultimately, the rupture between Armand and his parents. We have kept in regular contact with Yvonne and Maurice, as well as Robert and his family, but sadly, not with Armand.

There were other family ties between us. Ella, one of Papa's sisters, had married Oscar Bender, Aunt Yvonne's brother; Richard, one of Papa's brothers, had married Alice née Bender, a niece of Oscar and Yvonne. In fact, Maurice and Yvonne Steinberg were a pleasant couple and Mum and Dad got along well with them. Later, when I was a boarding at the student house of the *École des Hautes Études Commerciales* (HEC, in English, the School of Advanced Commercial Studies) in Paris, I joined them regularly for dinner in rue Lécluse, just a 20-minute walk away from the student house. They took the place of the grandparents I never had. As I knew Aunt Yvonne, with her practical sense she undoubtedly saw in me a possible advantageous match for her granddaughter Françoise. And at noon on Sundays,

I often went to have lunch in Colombes during the three years I studied in Paris, but the long-awaited rapprochement between Françoise and me never happened.

Although I do not at all remember the day that I saw Papa when he returned, I know from his accounts that the genuine silk stockings he had managed to get across the border were used to largely finance his travel expenses since they were a rare luxury in a France that lacked just about everything. We preserved Mum and Dad's ID photos taken right after the war. Every time I look at them, my heart hurts. Their emaciated faces reflect not only the hunger from which they have suffered constantly but also the anguish that did not let go for a moment during two years in hiding. Mum told me that after receiving a copy of these photos, my grandparents, uncles and aunts in Chicago were struck with such pity that for almost two years they regularly sent us parcels of foodstuffs still rare in France. I remember the joy I felt in opening each package when I found chocolate and chewing gum lozenges called "chicklets". The first exotic fruits, such as bananas or oranges, wrapped one by one in a kind of cigarette paper, had an unforgettable flavor, comparable to that of Proust's madeleine. In the end, I have kept happy memories of those four years of schooling at the rue Pierre Corneille municipal school in Lyon, especially of the last three years. As I was a pretty good student (except in arithmetic), I was left in peace. I got by, in the eyes of my teachers, for a student "applied", "studious" and not too "dissipated", according to the terminology then in use. I collected the "good points" and, better yet, the "testimonials" issued in exchange for accumulated "good points".

Each school year ended at the beginning of July. It was the summer vacation, the arrival of which triggered an explosion of joy in each of us students. We all sang then: "Long live the holidays, down with penances, and to Mr. or Mrs. So-and-so, a kick in the ass". We would then receive a vacation notebook, full of exercises, to fill out optionally. I remember having always had the most laudable intentions at the start of the holidays to live up to my reputation as a studious student. So, I put the precious notebook in a cupboard, telling myself that I had plenty of time, in two and a half months, to do all the suggested exercises. And each summer it wasn't until just 15 days before the start of the school year that I reluctantly pulled out the notebook to do just a few of them.

During these four years I had four different teachers: Ms. Dimet, whom I have already mentioned above, Mr. Besson, Ms. Vitton and Mr. Giraud. My preference goes to Mr. Besson because I felt he had a real affection for me which I gladly returned. I think I was what they used to call his "darling". Mr. Besson was particularly proud of me because I was very good at spelling.

1st year middle class: Mr. Besson on the left; I am in the 1st row, far right;
To my right, in the second row, my friend Pierre Charlet.

I remember a *dictation* test where Mr. Besson read a famous passage from Prosper Mérimée and we had to write it down. The passage was full of difficulties of all kinds, I succeeded in totaling the smallest number of errors. Because the teacher always complimented me during parent-student meetings, Mum and Dad felt flattered. He even suggested that he take me with him to a country house as the summer holidays approached. However, he was single, which made my parents reluctant. This is to my great regret because I felt in him an indulgence and a patience that I did not find in Papa.

From Mr. Besson's class I developed a love of reading. Our teachers encouraged reading at home. Once a week as a rule, the last afternoon was "library" time, and each student gave the teacher the title of a book he was to have read in the past week, and then read aloud the titles and the authors' names. Most of these books belonged to the Librairie Hachette publisher's "green library" collection of action and adventure books. This looked forward to this hour of happiness because books allowed me to dream, to escape the family atmosphere, sometimes made heavy by Dad's anger. Likewise, among all the study books distributed to us (free of charge) by the school, I gave priority to a book filled with excerpts from 19th and 20th century literature. This is how I came to know Hugo, de Maupassant and many others. I must have been seven years old when I got excited by an excerpt from Gustave Flaubert's *Madame Bovary* recounting Charles Bovary's comic beginnings at school, and asked Mum to give me "Madame Bovary" for the Christmas party marked by the distribution of gifts to me and all my little friends. Mom, who had no knowledge of French literature, went to the Lardanchet bookstore where she knew the saleswoman well, named Maria, an austere old maid. She pointed out to her in horror that this was a licentious book for adults only.

I was very surprised by this information and, above all, disappointed to be refused this gift. When I was finally able to read this novel, I came to the conclusion that at the age of 7, it would have bored me deeply and certainly could not have inspired in me the slightest perverse thought; there was absolutely no question or discussion of sex.

I had such a strong craving for reading that I devoured anything that came to into my hands. The fashionable collections of this time were: *Rouge et Or*; the series *Tales and Legends*; the collection *Sign of the runway*; and the collection *"Nelson"*. I think I have read the complete works of the Comtesse de Ségur (born Rostopchine), many adventure novels by Jack London, James Fenimore Cooper and James Curwood, most of the novels by Jules Verne and Georges Sand, the many works of Alexander Dumas, and the swashbuckling novels of Amédée Achard. Children's newspapers - commonly referred to as *illustrated* (now referred to as *comics*) – did not escape prominence in my imaginary world: *Les Pieds Nickelés, Gus and Gaétan, Bécassine, Spirou, Tintin, Superman, Zorro the Masked Avenger, Tarzan,* or *Big-Bill the breaker.* The liked best the latter, which appeared twice a month. Mom, always short of money, stubbornly refused to buy me this comic on the pretext that it was nothing educational. It was not a pretext; Mom was of course correct! But I didn't care because I was passionate about the adventures of this masked and muscular hero. Happily, Papa, who held the strings of the family purse, shared my taste for Big-Bill and allowed himself to be swayed, on condition that he read it before me…, I gladly conceded. I was also deeply fascinated by the world of magic, such as the stories in the *Fairy Tales of the Countess of Ségur* or in *Aladdin and the Magic Lamp*. I lose count of how many attempts I made to bring out the genius of Aladdin by vigorously rubbing all the lamps in our apartment. Alas, all without success! I was in dire need of a genius who would provide me with the pocket money to buy my comics and could help solve my arithmetic problems.

In addition to books, Mom and Dad would sometimes take me to the movies to discover Walt Disney's masterpieces: *Snow White and the Seven Dwarfs, Pinocchio, Bambi* or *Dumbo, the Flying Elephant*. The films I was excited about were those where pure and courageous heroes ended up triumphing over all obstacles. Thus *Robin Hood*, *The Three Musketeers*, and privateer or cowboy films, where the favorite actor was generally Errol Flynn.

It happened that Mum didn't want to leave me alone at home when she wanted to see a popular sentimental movie. So, she would take me with her. This bored me so much that I annoyed her several times during the film by asking "When are we going home?" Boredom even gave way to terror with a film in which Humphrey Bogart played the character of an assassin. I felt the same dread with the children's film *The Wizard of Oz*. This obsession with fear in the movies was usually followed by nightmares at night. This was the reason that, before each movie where Mum and Dad took me, I asked them to expressly promise me that I would not be afraid.

As for the initiation into classical music at this time of my life, I owe this to Papa and his violin. He would often boast that he learned to play after only nine months of lessons. Of his six siblings, only Aunt Liesel played an instrument, the piano. This musical gift came to them from their mother Emilie who knew how to play the zither. Though Mom had taken piano lessons as a young girl, but nothing came of it. In addition, she sang out of tune, which became a running theme of family jokes. Dad not only knew how to read scores, but he also played from memory various pieces considered to be great classics. The sound did squeal and scratch a bit, which was due to a lack of technique, but the notes were right. If I have been familiarized in this way with a few excerpts of this so-called classical music, it did not bother me too much. On the other hand, when I must have been eight or nine years old, Mum, probably at the instigation of her friend Simone, took me to my first opera. At that time, it was *Mignon* by Ambroise Thomas. Another time, it was *Carmen* by Georges Bizet. I felt such boredom, expressed in protests like "Will it end soon?" I had behaved like a spoiled child and was weaned for a long time from this type of entertainment!

Turbulent competitive games held little allure for me. Instead, my taste for reading very early on offered my imagination an unlimited field to travel and to experience feelings whose specific purpose seemed to be to make me vibrate; for this I owe Mum the cult of the book. She taught me to turn the pages carefully, without ever "cornering" them. As each school started, Mum would show me how to cover the class books with protective paper and to affix a label with the title of the book as well as my first and last name. Books were in general my only focus. So much so that when I went with Mum on a polite visit to one of her acquaintances, I quickly became bored listening to the conversations among "grown-ups". So, I asked Mum after arriving at the door to "...ask the lady if she has a book for me." Mum reproved me for what she thought was inappropriate. But in general, grown-ups were sympathetic to the little book enthusiast that I was, and I regularly got my book. I would sit in a corner and escape into a world of adventures, emotions and feelings. For me, it was the greatest happiness and satisfaction. The only book I remember Mum reading to me (I must have been five or six years old) was the Countess of Ségur's *A Good Little Devil*, about the poor orphan of Charles and her wicked aunt Mrs. Mac Miche. We even saw the play based on the book at the Théâtre des Célestins.

It was also through books that I had gotten as a child my deep and enduring attachment to the French language, as well as to this country which is my native France. One of these works, composed of two volumes, called *Childhood and the Life of Illustrious Frenchmen* was given me as a New Year's gift Mr. and Mrs. Joseph Pélisson (the same Pélissons that Providence had placed on our path to save us during the War)…), a tome each year. It is thanks to them that, still very young (I must have been only seven or eight years old), I discovered the existence of La Fontaine, Racine, Corneille, Colbert, Du Guesclin, Richelieu or Turenne… Subsequently, I had to force myself to realize that my mother country, in promulgating the Vichy racial laws, had with cowardly and ignominious indifference, denied my existence, and in fact had sentenced me to extermination for the sole reason that I was Jewish, that I was of Jewish parents. This explains the ambivalent feelings that I harbor about France: I feel a deep French cultural identity that no French anti-Semite can take away from me, even though over time, I have acquired my deep Jewish national identity, instilled by history.

During this period of five years, and until the Bar-Mitzva of my little brother Pierrot, we lived according to the rhythm of French secular traditions, including even the celebrations of Christmas and the secular New Year. Christmas was for me, the occasion to receive gifts. Dad even went so far as to disguise himself as Santa Claus, to my great delight. On the evening of December 24, the doorbell rang. Mom opened it and I saw, very impressed and with a pounding heart, the imposing Santa Claus walking in with a bag. In a counterfeit voice, he asked me then if I had been very good and if I had been a good student. On my affirmative answer, he then gave me various gifts and then left, saying that he still had a long way to go. "Why wasn't Daddy here?" I asked Mum. "Because he must have been running about at the last moment" she replied. It was only around the age of eight that one of my classmates said mockingly, "What, Lévi, do you still believe in Santa Claus?" I remember then feeling a terrible disappointment to see such a comforting illusion fly away. The best gift I received at that time was an electric train of simple manufacture (it was not a Märklin, far from it) of which I never tired. It made for my little brother Pierrot's happiness, and later still for that of my own eldest son Tamir. Perhaps it still exists among childhood relics that remain at the back of Maman's cupboards.

You are reading about my earliest memories, dating from 1944 to 1949, when we moved to 38 rue Raoul Servant and I entered the Lycée du Parc. This is the part of my childhood from which my earliest memories date. To complete the picture, I must evoke memories of the people, children, and adults who formed the backdrop of my life. With few exceptions, these were members of the Jewish community of Lyon. That is, they were survivors. As a child, it could not understand what a Jewish community meant, or even that the word "Jew" had at that time, strong pejorative connotations. But I did feel vaguely, without being able to explain it to myself, that we were different from other French people. The outward sign of this difference was clear whenever we went to a building called a synagogue (or shul) where we could hear a gentleman called a rabbi saying prayers in Hebrew, an incomprehensible language. I was (again) deeply bored in this "building". Inside, I had covered my head with a skullcap (commonly called a "keppele" or "keepah"). This keepah was to be quickly removed when leaving the synagogue; I sensed even then that we did this so as not to stand out. I remember feeling embarrassed at not being like everyone else, a feeling reinforced because my surname automatically revealed to my non-Jewish entourage, classmates, and teachers, that I was part of this different human group. A constant feeling of awkwardness led me to see myself in some way as stigmatized, as plagued in the eyes of non-Jews. I believe that this hampered any growth of self-confidence.

At home, our Jewish identity was reflected in the prayers that Papa chanted in Ashkenazi Hebrew every Friday evening and Saturday noon before and after the meal. I always feared, without daring to admit it, that as Papa,

Mama and I sang part of these prayers out loud, it would attract the attention of neighbors and would again, put us in danger. As soon as we returned to Lyon at the end of 1944, when I was five years old, every night before I fell asleep, Dad made me recite a short evening prayer, half in Hebrew and half in French. To this day I say this prayer every night, always before going to sleep. It is a custom I passed on to my sons and grandchildren. Such were the incomplete, imperfect, and negative, perceptions of Jewish identity of the child that I was. My enrollment in Talmud Torah classes in 1949, at the age of 10, only accentuated this perception and my unease since I was forced again to show myself as different from my non-Jewish comrades.

Because of their German origins, my parents befriended mostly German Jews, a matter of culture, no doubt. There were quite a few Polish Jews in the Lyon region, but my parents professed a certain condescension tinged with contempt when they spoke of them as *polnische yiden* or *polak*. So, from the age of five I very quickly became familiar again with German, though without speaking it. Although I spoke fluent German, my authentic mother tongue, until the age of three, Dad and Mum forced me to forget my German from 1942 on, so that I would not unconsciously betray us all to the Germans. From 1944 on, I also became familiar with the heavy German accent of German Jews speaking French. Subsequently, from the fourth grade to high school, I chose German to learn as my second foreign language, not out of any affinity for the language, but because I expected that it would be it easier for me to study. A few years later, I decided to alternate between studies of English and German, hoping to be able to handle each with equal ease. However, despite having a natural aptitude for both languages, along with good study habits, I never regained the command of German which I had once had and then lost in the two-year hiatus from 1942 to 1944. German had clearly passed, since those fateful years, from the status of mother tongue to that of foreign language.

My parents' closest friends were Fine and Albert Blum, a couple with no children. Albert was a good man, if a little clumsy, with a rather awkward sense of humor. On the other hand, Fine (diminutive of Delphine) was, as the name suggests, lively, expressive, mischievous, overflowing with humor and love of life, a person endowed with undeniable charm. I think she got me right and loved to make me talk about myself and my compatriots, even more if they were my friends. She knew everything about everyone and loved to promote this science in the Jewish microcosm of Lyon and its surroundings.

Then there were Ruth and Erich. The latter expertly managed a furniture business. He was a good man, moreover good natured, one gifted with a sardonic sense of humor who made cynically droll observations about nearly everyone.

Mom also befriended Lottchen (or Lottie, a diminutive of Charlotte), a slight woman as pretty as she was elegant, adored by her good doggie husband named Arthur, a sales representative who managed to practice his profession in France even though he never learned to formulate a sentence without stuffing it with more mistakes than it contained words. An artist of his kind! There were also Germaine and Robert, a mixed couple. Robert (alias Kurt), a Jew from Frankfurt am Main who had converted to Catholicism. Robert and Papa were both born on the same day of the same month of the same year (April 1, 1909) and both were also both gifted in bridge and music (Robert on piano and Papa on violin). Robert, a good-natured joker, who totally denied his Jewish and German origins to the point of converting, successfully ran a wholesale hardware business that brought his family a comfortable life. Germaine, who her husband called Manouche, died prematurely over thirty years ago while brother Robert, as I write these lines (2004), is happily turning ninety-five.

When I refer to my parents' "friends", I should rather use the term *acquaintances* or *associates*. My parents never had real friends in the community. It was an irony that their real friends were non-Jews: Marie and René Marcel from Toulouse, Margot and Raymond Gracia from St. Antonin or even Simone Garnier for Maman. Clearly, the Shoah and destiny had linked us so closely to the Marcels and the Gracias.

My Friend Pierre Charlet, 1946-1949

If I try to remember who my best friends were from that 5-year period, the name that comes to mind first is Pierre Charlet. It seems to me that it was during the 2nd year elementary course in rue Pierre Corneille in 1946 that I bonded with him following an incident that could have gone wrong. Unlike the previous year, when I had lunch in the school canteen, I would come home every day at noon for lunch. I would return for class which resumed from 2 p.m. until 4 p.m. or 5 p.m. The route home was simple: all you had to do was follow rue Bugeaud from the corner of rue Pierre Corneille and go up the street with your back to the Rhône. I crossed the busy Avenue de Saxe, then the square of the St. Pothin church, where I sometimes lingered to play marbles with my friends. The resulting delays earned me serious admonitions, sometimes accompanied by slaps, especially if I had kept Daddy waiting too long. I was always relieved when he was on tour for the day and did not come home at noon. I cannot remember how many times, when he *was* there, that the family meal turned into a personal nightmare because of the inquisition to which I was regularly subjected about my school activity. Feeling that I was on the dock, I quickly lost any words to answer Papa. He would raise his voice, my throat would tighten, it would end in tears, my appetite gone... In short, I felt tormented; I was not happy. I hasten to add that Dad was not a bad man. Far from it. But he was to me neither an educator nor a psychologist. He lacked the patience, indulgence, and loving encouragement that most children expect from a father. At the time, I was unaware of any insight that these attributes were ones sorely lacking in my home life, though there were some compensations from grand-parental affections.

So, it happened one day at the stroke of noon that I found myself with Pierre Charlet and some comrades. When an altercation suddenly split us into two groups, it quickly became so hostile that we ended up throwing stones at each other. One stone, which I had thrown, hit Pierre in the face. He ran away in tears, screaming that I had gouged out his eye. I returned home in a state of terror, not telling my parents a word about the incident for fear of punishment. After lunch I returned to school full of apprehension at the possible consequences of my actions. I could already see myself dragged in front of the dreaded headmaster and ordered to explain my reprehensible behavior. None of this happened. To my immense relief, Pierre reappeared with an adhesive bandage over his eyebrow arch. Feeling deeply sorry and chastened I told him that I hadn't meant to hurt him and that this would never happen again. A few days later, he invited me to play and have snacks at his place, probably on a Thursday afternoon. I told him that I was hesitant because I was afraid of being admonished by his parents. He swore to me that this would not happen.

Thus began a friendship of children that lasted until October 1949, when we moved to 38, rue Raoul Servant. He lived in rue Vendôme. When I went to his house, we would spend the afternoon playing goose or small horses on the large dining room table. His father, a silent man, worked as a watchmaker and repaired watches at home on a workbench near the window, in the brightest spot in the room. His mother, a very gentle woman, sewed and always spoiled us with a cup of latte with toast and a bar of Menier chocolate. There, with no questions about school, I was happy. Pierrot liked to show me his collection of miniature Dinky Toys cars of which he was very proud. At the end of the 1st year middle course, my parents decided, on the advice of the director, that I should sit for the entrance exam for 6th year in high school to continue my studies through the *baccalauréat* instead of the *certificat,* leading to a vocation, or trade. Pierrot Charlet chose the certificat path. This was in the same year (in October 1949) that we moved to rue Raoul Servant. This double-change of our schooling and neighborhood distanced us both in social status and geography. I must have felt some confusion, but these changes ended our friendship. At the time, I was more excited by the new start than I was sorry about the separation from with Pierrot.

While still living at rue Bugeaud my parents spent time with a German Jewish couple, the Francks who lived in rue Terme near the Place des Terreaux. This lasted until about

1948, the year that my one and only brother Pierre was born. The Francks had a son Claude who was my age. He was called Claudie, and we were to become playmates. Claudie was a very alert, boisterous, smart boy with great personal confidence, the kind of stereotypical son all young dads dream of, including mine of course. As for me, shy, awkward, dreamy, not fond of manual work, totally impractical, I was more fond of peace and quiet, taking refuge instead in an imaginary world inspired by my reading. As a result, I was often bullied by Claudie, who mockingly put me down, and who didn't hesitate to make me feel like I really wasn't "in the game". Very quickly, , I took an aversion to him and begged my parents not to visit these people because of Claudie. This aversion only became more unbearable when Dad took it upon himself, to cite him as some kind of example all the time. Instinctively, I felt that Papa, gifted with a practical temperament, did not cope well with my "gifts". Constantly rebuffed for what he saw as flaws, I gladly became taciturn in his presence. Mom on the other hand gave me the warmth and understanding that Dad couldn't show me.

My parents eventually accepted the fact of my repugnance towards Claudie and distanced their relationship with his family and stopped seeing them. Shortly after, Mom was shocked when, just after she had just given birth to my brother Pierrot at the *Sainte-Marguerite clinic*, by a visit from Mme. Franck. She had come not to congratulate her, but to overwhelm her with reproaches about some personal offense that she felt my mother had committed against her. This incident put a definitive end to any relations between my parents and the Franck family. I was greatly relieved. A few years later we learned from the community of the unfortunate, premature death of Claudie's father.

The Birth of My Brother Pierrot (Pierre), 1948

The birth of my brother Pierrot (Pierre Lévi) was certainly a milestone in the annals of our small family, though it did not much alter the course of my peaceful existence as a child. I was still eight years old when Pierrot was born on

April 7, 1948. The *Sainte-Marguerite clinic* was on the boulevard des Belges. This was just in front of the famous *Lycée du Parc* that I would enter eighteen months later. Like many of my friends, I was going to have a little brother, and an intruder, especially in Mom's life! Dad was often on the road, leaving Mom to parent the newborn. Indeed, I saw very little of him. Even when he was home, he hid behind the newspaper doing his crossword puzzles. My games, my books, my inner world did not appeal to him at all. I don't remember that he ever once decided to break down the parental barriers, erected between us for so long, even to take a walk with me (in the *Parc* for example). I wish that he would have taken a moment to listen to me, to be within my reach, to watch me patiently, to try and understand what made me tick as a child..., in sum, to help me gain confidence. I would have been so grateful to him. But Papa was so rarely there for me. It's probably not his fault; our temperaments were so different. It was only Mum who populated my childhood with what Papa could not give, and to whom all my affection went. The feeling that for so long prevailed in me about Dad was fear, the fear of his yelling, of his impulsive, even hysterical anger, and sometimes also the fear of blows. Although I was not a chronically beaten child, I knew what the slaps were. I became in the presence of my two parents (neither choice nor contradiction being allowed to me) a taciturn and withdrawn child, having learned that any revolt on my part would be punished. I lived with Papa's rebuffs, his unrelenting remonstrances about what he didn't like about me, my awkwardness attempting the slightest manual work, my too-pronounced taste for reading, my daydreaming, and my aversion to all forms of sporting or social activity... All this, not to mention that the stupid and meaningless comments on my report cards, saying "Could do better", were immediately interpreted by Dad as "lazy". In his eyes I was far removed from the prototype of the smart, rowdy, brawler, ringleader he'd dreamed of having. If at least I had had musical gifts like him, but again it was a total fiasco.

It must have been a huge disappointment for Dad. I can perfectly imagine that the arrival of Pierre promised to fulfill the expectations that his first-born son's personality had not met. Even though I was his son, the genes I inherited undoubtedly came from the Wolf side, hence from my maternal grandmother Grete, and even from my great-grandmother Oma Wolf, whose portrait adorns my childhood room at 38 rue Raoul Servant to this day. At each of my visits when I enter this room, my first glance is at Oma, where my gaze often lingers on hers, imbued with kindness, getting from her again and again affection and protection in the face of the trials that waited to confront me on my road.

Our Move to 38 rue Raoul Servant Lyon, 1949

I was ten years old when, in October 1949, we moved into our new apartment on the 1st floor of a new building at 38 rue Raoul Servant in the 7th arrondissement of Lyon. What a change from 69 rue Bugeaud, and in our life in general! On one hand, we were leaving a small apartment with no bathroom, no heating, and no WC (which was upstairs, with no flushing mechanism), in a 5-story walk-up with not a square of greenery nearby. On the other hand, we were moving to an apartment twice the size in a nine-story building, with four rooms, a balcony, a bathroom with a flush toilet, central heating, an elevator, and a roof terrace. The building, shaped like a horseshoe, enclosed a garden with stone benches and a sandpit.

It was reparations from Germany that had enabled us to take this leap forward. This seemed a gift from the sky. But at ten years old I did not really understand the value of this "gift", this quite inadequate recompense that my parents received in trade for the breakup of our families, the loss of my maternal grandparents at the end of their excruciating ordeal at the hands of the Germans and their Vichy collaborators, and my parents three years of nightmare, of anxiety and danger from 1942 to 1944.

Life in the new apartment was certainly a happiness of a sort, but one that was paid for dearly! In fact, throughout her life Mom will keep from the five years spent in our dovecote on rue Bugeaud the memory of true happiness, that of an end to fear, of the freedom and the joy of living rediscovered, that of no longer feeling the visceral anguish of hunger, cold and despair. Now older and wiser, as far as I am concerned, I see that the years 1942, 1943 and 1944 had marked us for life. Thereafter we would never again experience pure joy without a little voice somewhere within us whispering… "Remember".

The homes on the rue Bugeaud and neighboring streets were old two- or three-story houses best described as little more than poor old shacks inhabited by those who we would call "the little people", workers, artisans, petty officials. The language of their children was naturally vulgar, sometimes quite rude. Mum, who had grown up in an affluent middle class, suffered from this plebeian proximity and never missed an opportunity to emphasize to me the importance of being polite in language and manners. As I wrote earlier, some of my associates bothered her a lot and she asked me to space them out as much as possible. The move to rue Raoul Servant, moreover into a new building with modern comforts, meant for us a higher echelon in the social ladder and access to the life of the petite bourgeoisie. We saw this in the sartorial aspect of some of our new neighbors with the advent of ties and suits for men and more elegant dresses for women. The language of both adults and children was also more controlled and when necessary, chastised.

At first we rented the apartment at 38 rue Raoul Servant. Owned by a Mr. Dubreuil. Because Dad didn't want to be dependent on a precarious lease, he quickly offered to buy this flat from him. I was aware that the negotiations were long and laborious because Dubreuil's name kept coming up in my parents' conversations. Of course, the conclusion of the negotiations was in the end, favorable! It was ironic that some of the early owners of flats in our building were, like Dubreuil, workers. This was because the building was constructed to replace a collection of old houses that the Allied Air Forces had mistakenly bombed in May 1944, while aiming at the nearby railway line. The French state compensated several families who had lost their homes with an apartment that they could not otherwise normally afford. This level of comfort was so foreign to some of them that the toilet bowl quickly calcified without it bothering them in the least, and the bathtub served as a shed for storing apples harvested from land in the countryside!

My Return to the Sixth Grade, 1949

The return to school took place on October 1, 1949, at 7.45 a.m. I had turned ten years old just two months earlier. It was quite cold at an early hour on this autumn day. I can still see the group of children of which I was a part, bundled up in capes or coats carefully sealed with neck warmers, wearing berets, shod in galoshes for the most modest, satchel on their backs. We were clustered in a black mass in front the high school gate, just a few meters from the entrance to the *Lycée du Parc de la Tête d'Or*. There at the corner of boulevard Anatole France and rue Verguin we waited, not without some anxiety, for this gate to open, from where *The One* (Pardon me..., *The High School Student*) who would appear to kick off the first cycle of our future school career.

Ah, the magical sound of that word, whose deep meaning to my childhood ears at that time was akin to some inaccessible Olympus: *HIGH SCHOOL*. After the good news of my admission, based on the 6th grade entrance exam, Mum and I, during each walk in the Parc de la Tête d'Or, took care to pass the entrance on the side of the school in order to familiarize me with the sight of the venerable building which was to serve as my temple of knowledge. I beamed with happiness and pride and often repeated to Mom: "I will be a LYCÉEN ", then: "You can tell your friends: 'my son is a LYCÉEN' ".

We were making plans: "As soon as we receive the list of books and supplies, we will go and buy them at the *Parc* bookstore". More than half a century later, the bookstore still exists in the same location, at the corner of boulevard des Belges and Cours Vitton. Sometimes I linger in front of its window, not to read the titles of popular books, but to try to bring back the emotions of that past time when I knew this place as the source of the precious tools of my life, of my future "science". After we bought the books, a ceremony took place. With me at her side, Mum would cut into a ream of dark blue paper with a pair of large scissors, the exact portion needed to cover each book according to its size and affixing the label on which I wrote my name then "grade 6 B" under my name, and finally, below that, these three prestigious words: "Lycée du Parc".

6th B class - year 1949-50; Top row: 3rd from left (with glasses) Eisenkraft, then Appel, Rossel; 2nd row: Poulain, Colombe, Coster, Reboul, Blanchon; 3rd row: Boissel, Bourgoin, Roger, Hette, Leroy, Hinnen (the most gifted of us), Ginet, Drevet, Puignero, Dockès; 4th row: Fleury, Bernard, the author, Colombani, Lucien...

That year, in 1949, there were three 6th grade classes. I was assigned to 6th B, the program which included Latin. I seem to remember that 6th A included the study of Greek as well as Latin, a class attended by *elite* elements, according to prevailing opinion at the time. Despite multiple moves during my life, I have managed to keep this class photo. We were thirty-five students. My memory, which I question as I contemplate the faces of my thirty-five comrades one by one, agrees to give me twenty-two names. I consider myself satisfied that sixty-eight years later I still remember two out of three names.

Of these colleagues, I remember my impression that Hinnen was the most gifted of us, and that Poulain, the precocious son of a pharmacist, vituperated against Jews. I also recall Roger and that alas, his mother died just a year after this photo was taken. Finally, Eisenkraft was a fellow believer. Having heard my name on the first day in the school yard he approached and asked me in a low voice, "Are you a Jew?" And then, the same question from his neighbor on the right in the photo. Curiously, while looking at it, I remember that catechism classes were given at the lycée, an establishment which is supposed to be secular. During these classes, we Jews went to the "duty room" to free us from this "duty" and stigmatized our segregation.

The principal was M. Bobin and the assistant principal was M. Millot. The latter, a much-feared figure, was the embodiment of discipline. Each student caught in violation would come to him to duly record the sanction administered by the teacher whose said student had, wrongly or sometimes rightly, aroused the wrath. These two eminent figures sat near the main courtyard, elevated to the "Holy of Holies", to which student access was strictly forbidden. We were greeted in the first hour by our main teacher, Mr. André Daubard, who in the following grade also taught us Latin and French. The Latin textbook was by Gaston Cayrou and the French manual was by Chevallier and Audiat. I also had a Latin-French dictionary, the lexicon of Bornecque and Cauet that I had since the 4th grade, which was the *go-to* choice of French scholars of Latin. But the *Le Gaffiot* was the newer dictionary I used to the end of my Latin courses. I remember Mr. Daubard as an inherently good man with a strong sense of humor and as a teacher who truly loved us. It is surely due to his excellent human qualities as well as his pedagogical gifts, that he owed his position as our main teacher. Mr. Daubard awakened in me a real love for Latin, a passion for Roman history. Above all, he opened the doors of my already receptive imagination to the magical universe of mythology. So many names are jostling as I write these lines: Romulus and Remus, Numa Pompilius, the nymph Egeria or the goat Amalthea. And of course, there were the dramatic scenes depicted in engravings at the end of some of the chapters in the Latin textbook: the athlete Milo of Crotone, whose hand was accidentally caught in the crack of a tree and then attacked and finally devoured by a lion; Laocoön and his sons, suffocated by monstrous snakes emerging from the sea.

I still remember M. Daubard clearly announcing during the first Latin lesson that we would use the pronunciation known as "à la Française" and leave aside the so-called "restored" pronunciation. At that time, we got acquainted with the "1st variation", immortalized by Jacques Brel in his song *Rosa, rosa, rosam*. Enjoy a listen at:

Jacques Brel-rosa, rosa, rosam

After we had learned the first rudiments of Latin, Mr. Daubard firmly established his popularity on the day when, very seriously he wrote on the blackboard an apparently innocuous Latin sentence which he asked us to translate: *Cesarem legato alacrem eorum*. This puzzled us long enough until we noticed that our professor's face took on a smirk. A fellow smarter than the rest of us, finally realized that the expression, though meaningless, was a pun, a phonic play on the words *Cesar aime les gâteaux à la crème et au rhum* (Cesar likes cream and rum cakes!). A bit of nonsense that produced a general burst of laughter. Dear Mr. Daubard, I thank you with all my heart for the many good times spent during two years in your company and for making our "humanities" more digestible. This plunge into my childhood past also brings back to me a tragicomic episode, that I will recount after the next chapter, whose lesson led me to show some indulgence (and some mercy) when considering the relative importance of my own children's school marks.

The Talmud Torah, 1949

I was ten years old. In my parents' eyes this justified my starting course in Judaism in preparation for my future Bar-Mitzva. My non-Jewish 6th grade classmates were taking their high school classes as part of the official timetable. But Rabbi Poliakov from the Jewish community could not or would not demand that the high school start to offer a Talmud Torah course. As a result, I was forced to sacrifice all my Thursday mornings and Sunday mornings to learn

Talmud Torah on rue Montesquieu, half an hour by bus from home. I was relieved to finally do my Bar-Mitzva and finally sleep in twice a week! Nevertheless, Talmud Torah classes were fun and a chance to laugh with my young co-religionists. They were also how I got to know my first "love", with a certain Suzanne (Suzy) Samuel, whose family was originally from Colmar. Suzy made my lack of sleep more bearable. So it was that I learned the Hebrew alphabet and the Torah reading (which could not have been more boring). I was only interested in the Jewish history depicted by Gustave Doré: Samson, because of his Herculean exploits, especially excited my imagination.

My romance with Suzy had a sequel that emerged unexpectedly over the years. After a year of our romance, her parents decided to return to Colmar, a separation that hurt me deeply. Nine years later, in 1958, as a student at the HEC (*Ecole des Hautes Etudes Commerciales*, or the *High School of Commercial Studies* in English) in Paris, I was living at the Maison des Elèves (student housing) which hosted us provincials. There I befriended a Colmarian, Martin Karcher, with whom I am still in touch today. Recalling that Suzy had moved to Colmar, I tasked Martin to find the address of the Samuel family. Curious to know what happened to Suzy, a young woman now, I wrote to her. Her response surprised me by the firmness of her terms: she simply noted that my studies, which were exclusively secular, were an insurmountable barrier between us, since she was studying in an Orthodox Jewish institution in London. She concluded that it was better now that our contact should end. I didn't insist and concluded that we would never hear from each other again.

I Am Last in Geography Composition, 1950

Today I can smile at my memory of an incident that was to me a real tragedy at the time, revealing of the relationship that prevailed between my parents and me with regard to my high school studies. To understand it, you must take into account that Papa earned his living as a sales representative, with no other source of income. We were what at the time was commonly called a "humble family", and since studying was not a tradition in Dad's family, I had to live up to the financial sacrifices that my tuition fees represented; I was obligated to bring home, in return, results as brilliant as possible.

Fifth grade, 1950-51; the author is in the first row, second from the left

In October 1950, at the age of 11, I entered the 5th grade. Geography was taught by a good man, but in such a boring way that I neglected to work on it. During the 1st trimester the professor submitted us to several surprise written questions, without warning us that he would do so to check that we were studying his lessons regularly. In my case, the "proofs" were of course predictable. Taken by surprise, I handed over a weak effort, counting instead on catching up with the traditional quarterly composition which was usually announced to the students in advance. There were then another two or three surprise written questions and, each time, I handed in a frankly poor effort. Towards the end of the term, this teacher told us that there would be no quarterly composition and that he had already classified us based on the marks obtained on the prior written examinations. I was appalled at this very bad news. Then he read us the ranking, starting with the first. I secretly hoped that there would be a lot of comrades like me with even lower grades. We were about thirty students. As I had not yet heard my name after the twentieth name, I began to feel a vague, surging concern which grew more pronounced as more names were announced, but not yet mine. When I heard the professor proclaim: "Red lantern (the signal of the position of the last car on a train): Jacques Lévi", I suddenly felt the red of shame rising to cover my forehead. I remained glued to my seat, collapsed, not daring to look around me, convinced that all the eyes of my classmates were on me. It was the last hour of the morning. Slowly I picked up my things to put them in my satchel and slowly walked to the exit of the school. A single thought ran through my head: "How can I tell my parents the terrible news?" As usual, I went to the *Café du Parc* where Papa would be playing bridge, having planned to meet at the stroke of noon to "do his bridge" after making his representative rounds to various clients in the morning.

That was his conception of existence, how he would balance work and relaxation. His partners were always the same: Robert (Kurt) Linz, a Jew who converted to Catholicism through his marriage during the war to the daughter of a peasant woman from the region, Crombecque, another assimilated Jew whose original name must have been Krumbach , Julien Gintzburger, another Jew, but still a Jew. The 4th partner, Albert Wormser, was also a Jew, also assimilated, and of a rather crude mentality. He was well off, enriched by his trading in precious metals, and the husband of a charming woman, unfortunately childless. To digress a bit, one winter morning I was coming back from school and passing by the rue Ney, where the Wormser couple lived. Being in my path, Mrs. Wormser recognized me. Merciful at my chilled appearance, she ushered me into her apartment to serve me a hot drink, covering me with affection, maybe all the affection she wished she could have given to the child she could not have had. Unhappy in the household, she became the mistress of another celibate Jew, no doubt more attractive than her husband, named Sam Dreyfus, but who later abandoned her to marry a non-Jewish teacher…

Coming back to my personal drama, when I entered the cafe, I walked over to the table where the 'bridgers' were playing. One of them caught sight of me and called out in a distracted voice, before diving back into his cards: "So, my little Jacqui, how are you?" ". I didn't answer and stood there like a stick, hands at my side, my eyes lowered. The player who, according to the rules of this game, "played dead" (i.e., was the dummy) had time to look at what was going on around him. He saw my defeated face and, moved by a sudden solicitude, spoke to me in a pitying voice: "Well, my boy, that doesn't look right. Are you in trouble?" My father then lifted his eyes from his cards to look at me and say in turn, "Jacqui, what's wrong?" Under the puzzled gazes of the four players, I could not contain myself and burst into loud sobs before confessing in a hiccupping and broken voice: "I am last in geography composition ..." Except for my father, who was not the man to joke about the foibles of my studies, the bridge players burst out laughing. This news must have seemed even more comical to them since in their adult eyes it was only a minor, trivial event, and without any significance. Faced with this fit of mirth, Dad had no choice but to force himself to smile. I can only hope that after some reflection, these three bridgers will have understood that my despair actually reflected a child subjected to the strong tensions of parental demands and that it arose from a kind of mental cruelty by adults who are incapable of understanding the psychological fragility of their child.

I will insert not a digression, but an important parenthesis here. I cannot say it enough: materially as a child I never wanted for anything. I never went hungry, and was even showered with gifts, even if at the time they were modest. More important to me however, I never felt from my father the understanding and the indulgence that I thought would come from genuine fatherly love. In retrospect, it seems that he was incapable of seeing as positive, my unique potentials and nurturing them for their own sake, thereby giving me the personal assurance that it is so important to develop in any child. On the contrary, his tyrannical nature made me a fearful child, constantly anxious to avoid at all costs even the least conflict with him. He saw any resistance on my part as an attack on his dignity, allowing only for unrestricted submission. It seems` quite clear to me that my inability (or will) to resist my father's tyranny was all the more abetted by the development of my calm, dreamy and rather slow-paced nature.

Here we come to a fundamental problem of parenthood. Clearly, no parent is a born educator; this takes work. And no one comes to parenthood with an innate respect for a child's emerging personality. This typically requires a growing parental wisdom as a child matures. It may require advice or even professional training to understand clearly that a child is not the property of its parents. Everything follows from a basic truth: a child is a precious deposit that Providence entrusts to parents, and it is their responsibility to devote all their efforts to learn how to nurture the harmonious growth of this fragile plant. I am convinced that having grandparents (of which circumstances deprived me) would have mitigated the stress in our family relationships, helping to tamp down my parents' sometimes excessive (if not unfair) severity. And they may even have provided them some of the "growing wisdom". I remember that on the way home, my father, realizing my collapse and perhaps feeling judged by his friends as a hard father to his son, did not comment on the bad school news. As for me, the good marks I later received in most disciplines, including geography, suggest that I had learned a lesson from this bitter failure.

My Friend Alain Janconesco, 1952

Here is how I came to know my new friend's name. In October 1952 during the first class in our third year - our teacher asked each of us to introduce ourselves loudly and clearly by last name so that he could check us off on his list. When Alain's turn came, I heard not "Janconesco" but "Jean-Paul Escot", a very French name. I wondered, a bit annoyed, why the hell my new comrade would introduce himself with his first name as well. At recreation, he approached me and asked: "Lévi, are you a Jew?" I replied, instinctively on the defensive: "Yes, why?" "Well, me too." "How is that possible with a name like Jean-Paul Escot?" "But no, you mis-heard. My surname is Janconesco, a Romanian surname; my parents were deported.

Although the notion of deportation was at that time synonymous with misfortune, its true meaning was still very vague in my mind. Still, I was shocked by this revelation, one which brought me closer to him. We were both born in 1939, both Jewish and thus linked by a community of destiny. We became inseparable friends. For me this was unconsciously a source of great happiness because life in the Lévi house was far from breathing calmly towards me. Our friendship was for me a refuge where I could express myself freely, without constraint. Our phone conversations were endless.

Alain Janconesco

I learned, much later, that Alain had been miraculously taken in by compassionate neighbors when his parents Louis and Simone Janconesco had been arrested in the middle of the night by the French gendarmerie, as part of the *Vel' d'Hiv* (Winter Velodrome) roundup of July 16 and 17, 1942. They were deported by "Convoy 45" on November 11, 1942. Alain was then taken in by a Jewish communist couple who brought him up to his majority and ended up adopting him. This is how he passed from Janconesco to Horvilleur. By some unfathomable, to me at least, stroke of luck, Alain and his adoptive parents were never deported).

Alain lived in a very much politicized environment. He was thus my source of much historical information, for example, on the Dreyfus Affair. We had a real passion for the artists of the time: the singers Marcel Mouloudji and Francis Lemarque, and the singer-actor Fernand Raynaud, among many others. Learning from Alain, I developed my taste and love of the poets Charles Baudelaire, Arthur Rimbaud, and Paul Verlaine. He had learned some of their poems by heart. He transmitted this habit to me, and I set out to memorize many of those poems. I remember them to this day and have had the pleasure of reciting them to various French-speaking audiences in Israel. Our common course lasted three classes. The second part of the *bac* separated us, but we kept in touch. He went into medicine and later became a very famous homeopath.

At the time of our childhood friendship, we knew nothing about Vichy. Years later I sought and gained a deep knowledge of the martyrdom of the 320,000 Jews of the Jewish Community of France from 1940 to 1944. It seems to me that if, like my friend Alain, I had been orphaned by anti-Semitism I would have pursued all means to identify the main actors in the persecution of Jews in France, at the very least, to cry out my anger to them. Yes, we kept in touch episodically. But in all the time that I knew him, Alain preferred to remain silent about his personal drama. His parents had in fact been deported to Auschwitz, never to return.

Alas, he died prematurely in 2012, and to the end, under the influence of his Communist guardian, he stood firmly on the sidelines of his Jewish identity which remained devoid of any significance to him. This is something that still saddens me when I remember my friend.

Edmond Rivet, Teacher of My Second Class, 1953-1954

I had just turned 14 when I entered 2nd class in October 1953 when the average age of my classmates was around 15 or 16. Our class had twenty-six students, all boys of course as was the custom of the day. I gaze at the faces of my classmates, one by one, in the class photo below.

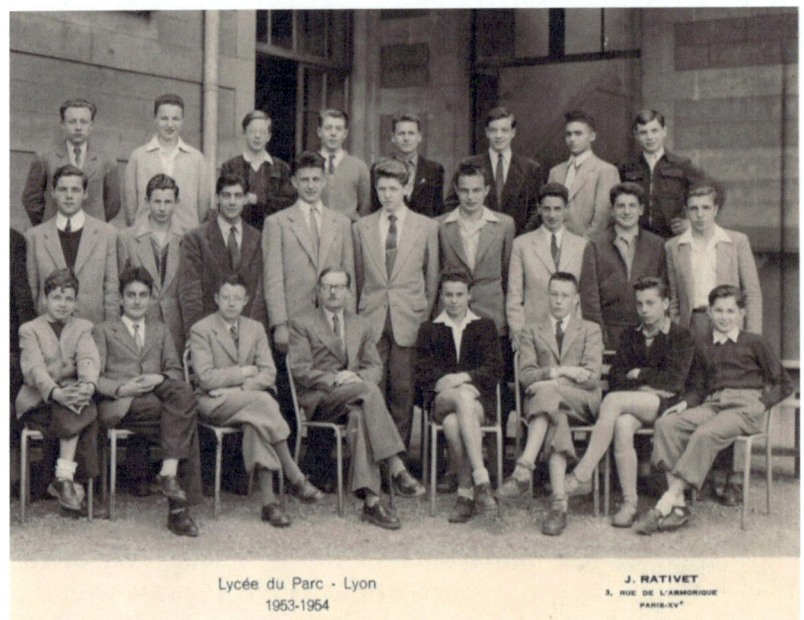

Fifth grade, 1953-54: From left to right, 3rd row: Touzet, Millot (the son of the formidable censor of our school), ?, Journoux, Lapandéry, ?, Colomb, my friend Alain Janconesco; 2nd row: ?, ?, Buisson, ?, Sölke, Colombet, Sautour, Belin, Plassard; 1st row: ?, Reveret, ?, Professor Edmond Rivet, Belloour, Colombe, Bouffanet and, last but not least, me.

Many of us already wear ties, making us look like grownups in the photo. What is striking, despite the austere look on our teacher's face, is the impression of happiness and fulfillment in most of our smiling faces. At any rate, it is genuinely so at my seat! Never again, neither in earlier class photos, and nor in later ones, will I wear such a happy expression as did that year. As is the case with others class photos I have kept in a box to this day, some names still are question marks, details refusing to surface. I do remember that Raymond Bellour stuttered, but that when he appeared on a theater stage, the stutter disappeared.

By tradition, the first hour of the first day of class consisted of introductions to (and from) our head teacher. I learned his name, Edmond Rivet, for the first time from my own classmates. Although I had attended this high school since my 6th year, I had not heard of him because he didn't teach the 1st cycle classes that we had just finished, and because I knew none of the upper classmen with whom to exchange impressions of our respective teachers.

Mr. Rivet was a short, thin man, whose glasses concealed a lively gaze. Outwardly he projected a dignified, sober elegance that at once inspired a respect which was confirmed and amplified from his first words. A firm authoritative voice, embellished with humor, captured our attention. It was clear that we were dealing with a true professional..., a real teacher. In fact, whatever learning we may have predicted for his class was an underestimate: we had hit the jackpot. I don't remember, during my entire school career, having waited so impatiently for lessons from Mr. Rivet. From day one, all my conversations with my parents were marked by "Mr. Rivet said...".

He exerted on me the influence that Augustin Meaulnes had on François in Alain-Fournier's 1913 novel, in that he brought me into the new world of 19th century poets, notably Verlaine and Rimbaud. I remember learning with such pleasure Verlaine's "The Art of Poetry". A stay in Haute Provence gave a very particular flavor to the last stanza of this poem: *May your verses speak of fortunes/ And to stiff morning breezes/ spreading fresh aromas of mint and thyme.../ All the rest is literature!* This same Haute Provence was the Rimbaud's ideal place in which he set two others of his "diamonds": *Roman* (*Novel*)and *Les Reparties de Nina* (*Nina's Replies*).

My inner world was literally upended by these discoveries. That year, these two poets became my best friends, followed a few years later first by Baudelaire and then by La Fontaine. The last is traditionally. and wrongly I believe, reserved for children in the lower grades. The verses of all these poets are forever in my memory and I say them always with the same delight. They live in my personal garden, and I owe this rare pleasure to my wonderful Mr. Rivet. On my hikes in nature, I can proudly address myself to nature, my indulgent audience, declaiming my friends' verses for hours without costing me the slightest effort. But now, let's come back to Mr. Rivet's engaging style of teaching.

I remember well an anecdote he told us to illustrate the genius of the child prodigy Arthur Rimbaud, who was a student at the Collège de Charleville. The principal knew Arthur's exceptional talent and his ability to compose Latin verses with dexterity. So, he decided to enter the Collège into the Academic Competition in this discipline, certain that the performances of his young foal would bring fame to his establishment. The contest took place on July 2, 1869. It was to last from 6 a.m. to noon, with each contestant to present a poem in Latin verse whose subject had been curtly titled "Jugurtha". More than an hour after the start of the competition, the supervisor in the room where Arthur was waiting his turn came in dismay to the headmaster to tell say that the teenager, in whom the college had placed all its hopes, had yet to write the 1st line of his composition. The worried headmaster rushed to Arthur's room: "Well, Rimbaud," he said, already disappointed, "what's the matter with you?" Arthur glared at him and shouted angrily, "I'm hungry!" The principal quickly gave orders for a solid snack to be served to his prodigy, who hastened to do it justice. This meal finished, Arthur composed, in no rush and with ease completing his eighty or so Latin verses. From the pen of the young Rimbaud, King Jugurtha predicted the defeat of Abd-el-Kader, his imprisonment, and his release by Napoleon III. The meal served to the starving young man must have been particularly tasty because Rimbaud won 1st prize in the Academic Competition.

I know now that storytelling and anecdotes like this colorful one, brought us much closer to Rimbaud and to true learning... much more than a cold, dispassionate lesson could ever have done. Furthermore, in contrast to the cramming for exams in the 1st class, there was no end-of-year exam hanging over the 2nd class, so we could grow and learn in a spirit of total relaxation. For all these reasons, the year 1953-54 will remain to me in retrospect the summit, the respite, the year of great joy of learning, indelibly linked to the endearing Mr. Rivet.

Strangely enough, I never saw him again, although I stayed at the Lycée du Parc for four more years. But perhaps not so strangely; at that time teachers and students were kept at a great distance. It did not help that I suffered from a great shyness which took years to lose. The school itself had no informal framework to bring at least an annual rapprochement between teachers and students. I am sure that, shy or not, I would have taken advantage of such a chance to tell him with what pleasure I thank him for teaching me and for the pleasures I took in exploring and discovering new authors. I would have wanted him to know how much I appreciated him, especially at an age when I still lacked confidence and could have used a guide on the path of this existence which so scares young people.

I know that I would have consulted with Mr. Rivet about whether to pursue further higher studies in a regular college of arts and sciences (the *École normale supérieure, or "Normal Sup"*), or in a business college (the HEC, or Hautes Études Commerciales)? Without this consultation, I opted for HEC. Was my "choice" just the flip of a coin, an accident, a mistake? Looking back, that I know myself better, I should have pointed myself (or been pointed) towards the *Normale Sup*, maybe to study drama! I wonder now how I admired M. Rivet but did not then recognize a man endowed with charisma and true acting talent. As a true teacher, he had developed the art of using the power of the verb, of gestures, of action, and of the fire in his eyes to introduce us to all the literary geniuses he wished us to know. In the field of education as in politics there is a great deal of theater whose purpose is to engage and seduce an audience. And Mr. Rivet's audiences, we *seconds* and the generations of students in the 2nd classes who preceded and followed us (including my young brother Pierre), were indeed irresistibly and lastingly seduced.

Ten years then passed. My studies and the military service completed, I was alone with myself in Strasbourg, able to measure myself against the beginnings of my professional life. Despite the turmoil of a busy social life and still single, I had enough time to reflect on the trajectory of my life. And in such times, I would sometimes remember the one adult, thanks to whom I had have and keep my love of French and foreign literature and the tools to judge a work. I realized one day that the least I could do was to say thank you to Mr. Rivet for his part in my development. Thus, one evening in 1964 when I felt myself embraced with nostalgia for my high school years and a deep gratitude and affection for my favorite teacher, I decided to write and tell him so. Mr. Rivet was then approaching retirement. The emotional terms of his response touched me deeply and showed me that I was right to take this initiative.

The Year of the 2nd Baccalauréat, 1955-56

Examinations that took place over two years in the lycée were at that time called the *Baccalauréat* (or *bac* for short). The first examinations came at the end of the first class. To prepare for the 2nd part, the pupils had to choose between three options called elementary mathematics, experimental sciences, and philosophy. I knew that I was not good at math, and I did not feel any inclination for physics, chemistry and other exact sciences. So, with my obvious lack of maturity, I opted for philosophy, not suspecting that this choice would doom me to failure. Thanks to family relations, and myself a dreamer, ill-tutored in the handling of ideas, I had yet to learn the art of abstract thinking, a field that feels foreign to me to this day. No wonder the marks I got for the assignments I handed in were so terrible. And that of course led to my fear of bitter failure in the *Baccalauréat* exams.

It was in this state of deep frustration, expecting this failure that I fell sick in May 1956 in the middle of a philosophy course. Unable to stand it any longer, I asked the professor for permission to go home. I wanted only one thing: to lie down on a bed. Once I got to home, I found the door closed and my mother out. I went downstairs to the concierge, Mme. Ville, who saw how extremely pale I was. She immediately made me lie down on a sofa. As soon as my mother returned, she sent for a nearby doctor who was unable to diagnose my condition. I was vomiting and had a high fever. The next day, after a restless night, our family physician, Dr. Charles Franck, came to examine me. He was also puzzled, seeing in me no symptoms of a classic illness. He then summoned another doctor who in his turn was also unable to make a diagnosis, and who limited himself to writing a report. On the 3rd day, foreseeing that the following day would be the feast of Pentecost and seeing the strong deterioration of my condition, Dr. Franck, who had become very worried about me, brought in a well-known surgeon, Professor Peycelon.

When Franck wanted to show him the faculty professor's reports, Peycelon threw aside these papers with a sudden gesture and demanded: "Show me the patient!" After a brief general examination, he did a digital rectal exam which made me scream in pain. "Appendicitis!" He decided that I must be at once admitted to the Red Cross hospital. This appalled and frightened my parents. Mum burst into tears, believing me to be lost. "Don't worry," said Peycelon, "I will save him for you." That same evening, I was operated on, with my surgical wound packed with copious amounts of antibiotics to neutralize the possibilities of infection.

I especially remember feeling an intense thirst and that I was strictly forbidden to drink. I was only allowed to moisten my lips with a wet cloth. After a few days, when I was finally allowed to drink, all feeling of thirst was gone. I was barely saved from a very nearly fatal sepsis. It took me weeks to recover.

To speed up my recovery my parents decided to send me to a youth center, called "Le Galizon", in the Alps, in Villard de Lans, run by the Bonnet family. There I spent three weeks of absolute rest in a magnificent natural setting offering an endless number of mountain walks. I bonded with Francois, one of the Bonnet sons, a jovial boy with whom I enjoyed chatting. He was a history student at the faculty of Grenoble. His sister Alice, nicknamed Loulou, was about ten years older than I, petite with long black hair and a sparkling look of mischief. Needless to say, she made a deep impression on me. I confess that I fell madly in love with her. As shy as I was at 17, I hid my feelings and she realized none of them!

Almost fifty years passed when in 2005, when I was staying in Lyon with my ninety-one years old Mum, I made an excursion with a couple of friends, France and Ronald, in the Alps. On the way back, we stopped at Villard de Lans. I asked a shopkeeper if he knew of a Loulou Bonnet in the village. It turned out that she still lived in this village. I went to her address. Despite the years, Loulou still had the same lively eyes. For an hour we took great pleasure remembering my summer of 1956 at the "Le Galizon" youth center. Once again, I was reticent, and did not mention the tender feelings that she had inspired in me then.

I come back now to the Baccalauréat exams. Once I had recovered from my operation, my parents enrolled me in a 1956 summer course to prepare for the catch-up session of the *bac*. To my good fortune, I met excellent professors of philosophy and history who, with a simple but effective pedagogy, restored the requisite confidence in my abilities so that I was able to obtain the coveted bachelor's degree in September of the same year. Nevertheless, still at age seventeen, I was sorely lacking competent institutional (or any other) vocational guidance that could have detected my true aptitudes and that would have helped me to avoid the errors of referral and judgement that were the cause of much suffering that followed. As we will see later, it took another thirty-three years for me to emerge from the consequences of these errors.

An Interlude of First Love, 1956-1958

The August 1956 *vacation course* for the second session of the *bac* was held on the rue Louis Blanc in the sixth district where I had grown up. Zimmerman was the philosophy professor. From him I acquired a simpler, less abstract vision (and a better understanding) of the subject than I had gotten from Jouguelet, my first philosophy professor. This of course restored my self-confidence.

My greatest revelation came from my history and geography teacher who taught us how to approach in a methodical way, any subject according to an easy-to-memorize logical diagram. All lessons were mixed gender, which was a novelty for me because studies at the Lycée du Parc were reserved for boys (the Lycée Edgar Quinet was for girls). After the first day of the philosophy course, we all met in the reception room. It was then that my gaze fell on a young brunette girl, smiling and engaging. Right after we introduced ourselves to each other, We began a conversation, and it immediately became apparent that we had much to talk about. Her name was Jacqueline Terrier, and each exchange between us gave me real pleasure. Once the morning lessons ended, we went to a nearby cafe and after only a few moments, I felt certain that I had found the girl of my dreams. She had a natural warmth, quick wit and enthusiasm that immediately won me over.

Sixty years later, it is difficult for me to reconstruct the feelings that gripped me then, but they were certainly intense and overwhelming. We exchanged glances that left not the slightest doubt about the sudden feeling that had seized us. A reciprocal magnetism had violently attracted us to each other. No doubt Cupid's arrow had pierced us with deeply.

Thus began a relationship, an unforgettable adventure, and the creation of an unforgettable memory. We two were enthralled, enchained even, by that feeling of the kind of happiness one only experiences in true "first love", a feeling that you experience once in a lifetime. We did not (at least I did not) know how to develop this burning passion. I remember walking with her in the *Parc de la Tête d'Or* in a natural setting that surrounded and enhanced our feelings. Sitting on a bench I moved to kiss her. It was my first time kissing a girl and had no idea how to go about it. Courageously I put my mouth on hers. As our teeth clashed lightly, I told myself that it was much less pleasant than what I had seen in the cinema. This is how we found ourselves in the role of lovers kissing on a public bench dear to the poet and songwriter Georges Brassens.

Burdened by an excess of pusillanimity stemming from my education as a boy "as it should be", I at first struggled terribly to ignore the looks of strangers strolling by…, to not *"give a damn about the sidelong gaze of honest passers-b*y". But, little by little we improved our technique and soon, it was like in the cinema, if not better. You too can listen to Brassens' song of "The Lovers Kissing on a Public Bench" at the following link below:

Les Amoreux des Bancs Publics

I didn't dare introduce Mlle. Terrier to my parents, but they knew... My mother told me later that, out of concern, Papa followed us at a distance for fear that I might do something irreparable, like stepping into a hotel room. I craved to but again, didn't dare. My education and reality stopped me. Those days spent together on vacation passed like a dream. Then came exams for the second session. I was received, she was not. She had to retake her philosophy class. Her parents enrolled her in school in Villefranche, 35 km from Lyon; I enrolled in the HEC exam prep course at the *Lycée du Parc de Lyon*. I visited her once or twice and, in our separation, we exchanged much mail vibrating with love.

One day when I was visiting, we finally approached the prospect of a future together. Being resolutely faithful to my Jewish identity and planning to live in Israel, I told her that she would have to consider converting to Judaism. I said that living in France with my surname meant being the constant butt of widespread anti-Semitism with which I had no wish to always measure myself. She exclaimed: "Why convert me and, moreover, ask me to go to live in a country which is totally foreign to me?" I had to explain: "If we get married without you converting, our children will bear my name, but born of a non-Jewish mother, they will not be Jews, only to suffer in France for no reason other than having my Jewish surname. Above all, I told her that I was proud to be Jewish and that I wanted my children to share my identity without reservation. Finally, I shared the concern that many Jewish parents share with their children: imagine a Jewish man, married a Catholic woman with whom he had children, none of whom were raised Jewish. One his sons, finding out he was Jew, called his father a "dirty Jew" in a fit of rage. If I were that father, I would have been devastated by a terrible, inconsolable loss. Finally, we were forced to realize that we had reached an ideological impasse and that we could only continue our journey separately. It was a bitter-sweet conclusion to the wonderful moments that we had spent together. While the end was sad and bitter, later the memories are sweet.

My Studies at the HEC, 1958-61

My class of 1961 began in October 1958. I had just turned 19. I was *one* of the youngest but not *the* youngest entrant. The oldest was Raymond Prayer (from the commune of Bourgoin in the French alps), who had passed the entrance exam after just one year of preparation. He was a nice, modest, working-class boy. Although we were close at the time, we didn't keep in touch. The HEC (*L'Ecole des Hautes Etudes Commerciales*) was a Paris Chamber of Commerce flagship, a nursery for "papa's sons" and so, a school for training the successors of bank managers and company CEOs. HEC students were given the nickname "fistici" (a contraction of "fils est ici", meaning my "son is here"). A famous "non-fistici" exception was Paul Reynaud, Prime Minister of the *Third Republic* who resigned after failing to save France from German occupation at the start of World War II. Dominique Strauss-Kahn is a more recent exception. An economist, he was a socialist minister in the Jospin government and head of the International Money Fund (IMF). He became embroiled in sexual scandal, losing a chance to run for president of France!

Until 1964, the HEC was in the 17th arrondissement near Parc Monceau, on boulevard Malesherbes next to the Malesherbes metro station. We "provincials" lived in the *Maison des Elèves*, a 5-story student housing building that could be accessed through an underground passage from inside the school. Because the HEC is a private school, the cost of study, room, and board was a considerable financial sacrifice for my parents, given their modest income. It would have been far less costly if I had done my studies at a provincial business school such as the *Ecole Supérieure de Commerce* in Lyon. However, the prestige of having their son study at HEC was such that my parents willingly accepted this financial burden. I did not thank them enough, if only for the personal confidence and social status that the HEC diploma conferred, and the doors that it opened to me and thorough which I later passed.

Zin all, our class had some 300 students, Parisian and provincial, the former showing overt condescension to the latter. Many of us provincials lived at the *Maison des Elèves* because it was so convenient to the school. Each *Maison* student had his own room. A "room boy" was responsible for cleaning the rooms and making the beds, testimony to the high social status to which HEC students had arrived. But the five-story building had no elevator. First year students lived on the upper floors. The following year, as second year students, we moved down one or even two floors, depending on availability. As is typical for such institutions, the food for all was detestable, so much so that very quickly, our pocket money was spent on restaurant meals. We discovered that the best restaurant in the neighborhood was, "Le Petit Périgord" whose *paella valenciana* made us quite full and happy.

The Parisian students had cataloged students from the provinces as second-class citizens, ignorant of the refinements of the capital. But, from the start of our HEC tenure, comradeships, memories, and even real friendships, formed based on common tastes and cultures and backgrounds. I remember Alain Tessier in particular, originally from Nantes, whose pestilential socks made everyone run. He was unrepentant in his pursuit of girls, and he regaled us with countless tales of his amorous exploits. I also remember Alain Rozan, a pleasant redhead from Nevers, always smiling, very affectionate and ready to help, and who most unfortunately became handicapped by polio that he contracted during our stay. Finally, there was Martin Karcher, originally from Colmar, with whom I surprisingly found myself hooked. I liked him because of his serious, poised, thoughtful way of approaching life. He analyzed everything from a dry, logical perspective. Already, by his demeanor and posture, one sensed that he had both feet planted in the ground, a 'solid tree', little inclined to emotions. His speech was slow; I felt that each word was passing through a sieve of judgment, each weighed carefully before spoken. His writing, above all, struck me with its great regularity, an adult's writing, neither impromptu, nor imprecise or impulsive, and without inappropriate surprises that characterize less practiced writing. Given my inclination to dream, fondness for poetry, and a head stuffed with literary memories, Martin's writing was to me as ballast, bringing me back to reality. We were both sons of modest means, part of the same social milieu. Our similar social environment and German background erased all other borders. Above all, he did not harbor any of the anti-Semitic prejudices that I experienced in so many of my classmates in Lyon. We quickly became an inseparable pair. Together we set out to discover Paris. By "discover" I mean that we shared our impressions and what we felt during visits to historical monuments, museums, or other sites in the Paris region. We passionately discussed the films of the day, including those of Ingmar Bergman or Alfred Hitchcock, as well as the old classics by Marcel Carné, Robert Bresson or René Clair. I especially remember that after the evening meal, we would walk along the rue des Dames to the avenue de Clichy. On our walks we endlessly discussed the day's events and, moved by our mutual Parisian and other inspirations, made plans for rural or Parisian weekends. We understood each other well, and that gave me an extraordinary feeling of well-being. I longed in secret to find this same bond with a girl but then, such a windfall never presented itself, though not for want of searching ballrooms, clubs, public gardens, and cafes!

At the HEC I developed an ease in establishing social contacts. As a result, and thanks to a recommendation from Renée Sternheimer, a friend of my parents and president of the Women's International Zionist Organization of Lyon (the WIZO Lyonnaise,) I met the Cerf family. They lived in the 16th arrondissement of Paris, and when I presented myself on the phone, I was invited to come for a Shabbat supper on a Friday evening. Excited by the prospect of introducing myself into the good Parisian Jewish bourgeoisie, I went to 48, rue des Belles-Feuilles, a street whose very name (*beautiful flowers*) was a happy omen). In spite of myself, I was dazzled by an apartment furnished in exquisite taste and by the cheerful, affectionate warmth with which Mme. Juliette Cerf welcomed me. Mme. Cerf introduced me to her husband Robert Cerf, her mother, Mme. Minkel, and her children, Jacques, Bertrand, and Annie. Jacques, the eldest, was already well-established in the working world; Bertrand, a year older than me, was a student in the first year at the École *Supérieure de Commerce de Paris*; and Annie, called Nanou, was a high school student about sixteen years old. Once at the table, I was struck by the dinner, a meal where the men remained in jackets carefully buttoned in the middle, with service provided by a stylish Spanish maid, Aurora. Table-conversation was marked by restraint, a refined politesse, and good humor. This even tenor of conversation seemed essential. I could not imagine that, following an unexpected comment or interjection, anyone at the table would have indulged in unalloyed, side-splitting laughter. No, no! Self-control was the order of the evening; only a slight smile was allowed. The meal, however excellent it was, must in no case engender comment, never mind a show of sensual enjoyment. It would have been considered improper. The meal was to be a pretext for a conviviality allowing a conversation but not beyond what seemed to me then, a regrettable contingency. For me, accustomed to a more needy, petit bourgeois temperament, with other aspirations other than material well-being, it was a great novelty to enter an elevated social sphere. Its novel habits and customs should over time henceforth take the place of my model and adjusting my own aspirations.

Today, with hindsight, I acknowledge that I could not have fallen into a better family where I found all the emotional and moral comfort that I, a young, isolated student in Paris instinctively sought. It was quickly obvious to me that Mrs. Cerf was the pillar and strength of this family by virtue of her radiant personality, her human warmth, her communicative enthusiasm, and her fundamental optimism.

Already at the time she suffered from defective vision, but she hardly ever spoke of it. I had been present at the funeral of her mother, Mme. Minkel. I saw Mme. Cerf after the death of her husband Robert, and again many years later, when Nanou died under tragic circumstances. Mme. Cerf was then living in a fine apartment on avenue Bugeaud, which had become too big for her alone. Despite her age and being in mourning, the timbre of her voice had not changed. She welcomed me each time with her affectionate warmth. She suffered greatly because of the accidental death of her daughter Nanou, who was her most intimate confidante and her great support after she had become a widow. Her loneliness and the depth of her anguish gripped my heart. On a mission in Paris on behalf of the KKL in the 1990s, in the last years of her life, all I could do was to phone her. Any visit should receive, according to her, the prior approval of Jacques who, no doubt for good reasons, did not give it to me. I lamented this loss because Mme. Juliette Cerf had become like a second mother to me.

In retrospect, I feel like I was adopted by the Cerf family, in part because of the mutual affinities that Bertrand and I discovered. We were same age, with the same community affiliation, and we shared a similar course of studies. Most important, we shared a taste for the arts even more developed in Bertrand, who had grown up in a family atmosphere strongly steeped in culture, nurtured by a great openness to the outside world. I appreciated his exemplary modesty (a trait raised to the level of a religion) and above all, a remarkable sense of humor. Without realizing it, I continued to thrive away from a harsher existence, within the protective environment of the school, surrounded by the affection of friends such as Bertrand and his family. The three years of study led me to discover the wonders of Paris, I could not know then that what I learned was to be of great use to me some thirty years later, when I became Delegate of the KKL in Paris. It was a reprieve that ended when my military service began.

The contours of my personal and professional future were still vague at the end of my stay in Paris, but it was during that stay that I had a first inkling that Israel might play a role in my life. One day in our class auditorium, I was speaking about Israel with a classmate when another named Ajenstat, sitting in front of me, turned to say that he had a HEC comrade from an earlier class, Gérard Lévi, who lived in Israel that I could contact for a possible stay. A few moments later at recess, I asked Ajenstat why *he* was interested in Israel, he replied with a smile: "I am also a Jew too; My name is a francization of Eisenstadt." Three years later, I wrote my first letter to Gérard Lévi. He was quick to answer me, encouraging me to move to Israel, to make my Aliyah. I was still far from being ripe for a first visit to a country that I knew nothing about. I had to wait another five years to decide on this visit.

Finding Israel... and Sarik, 1956-1967

My story with Israel begins in the summer of 1956. At that time, my knowledge of Israel was virtually zero. In fact, my understanding of Israel's history remained close to nil for a long time, even after I had settled there. That is the year of my peritonitis operation, just two months before turning 17. This is what prevented me taking part 2, the Philosophy Section, of the baccalaureate exams. As I wrote a few pages ago, my parents enrolled me in the preparation course that allowed me to attend a remedial course in September..., to avoid losing a year. It was during this remedial course, while chatting with a classmate, that I had a premonition of my Aliyah and future in Israel.

Any logical, objective consideration of how my future would unfold would have kept me rooted in the country where I had grown up and studied, and whose language was thoroughly mine, and whose French mentality was mine. Clearly, I was a product of French education, strongly imbued with French culture. I should, by rights, have remained an authentic Frenchman. And this would have been so had the circumstances of my youth, of my early childhood, remained a mystery to me. But they did not. From what my parents revealed to me, I came to understand that being Jewish in France created an insurmountable gap between my compatriots and me.

My Aliyah project lingered for eight years in all, from 1958 when I began my studies at HEC. It began in earnest when I learned of Gérard Lévi (HEC class of 1956), by then living in Jerusalem, with whom I had begun a correspondence. I still have one of his letters that provided the encouragement that I needed to move beyond an early premonition. The lingering continued through my French military service from November 1961 to May 1963, and then in the next two years in Strasbourg, and, finally in Paris in March 1966. So, I had had ample time to reflect on the pros and cons of Aliyah. In 1965 I took my first serious look at experiencing Israel. I had learned that an emissary from the Jewish Agency responsible for the Aliyah of the young, Shimon Hadar, was due to visit to the Jewish Community Center of Strasbourg in January. When we met, he offered me a 6-month stay at Kibbutz Sarid in the Galilee near Migdal Haemek, in the Jezreel Valley. I said to Shimon "6 months! that seems very long to me". "Not at all, you are young, single and that is the length of time necessary for a good understanding of the country and its inhabitants" he replied. I accepted, and we agreed that in a few months I would receive a boat ticket to Haifa, along with and all necessary instructions for my trip to Kibbutz Sarid. But "a few months" passed without a word from Mr. Hadar. In June, without the assistance of the Jewish Agency, I decided in desperation to go to Israel at my own expense. It was a 6-week trip that I made with two friends, one of whom brought along his convertible Peugeot! Before we left, I arranged a work engagement in France to begin upon my return. Of course, as soon as I arrived in Israel in July, I had a message from my parents that the famous Shimon had finally deigned to contact me to execute the project agreed to seven months earlier. Too late! That episode says a lot about the seriousness of the Jewish Agency, or at least of its representatives at the time!

Nevertheless, his negligence that ended one project led to another that changed my destiny for the better. As it happened, every day in Israel was a wonder for me, a chance to experience the beauty of the land, the contact with, and warmth of the inhabitants, and even just hearing the spoken Hebrew language. Among other travels in the land during that short visit, I spent nearly ten days at Kibbutz Houlata where I made friends with other young people my age. Israel's charms worked their magic on me for these six weeks. One of the most important awakenings was the realization that my Jewish identity made me a full Israeli. This was just the medicine to a cure the "ashamed Jew" disease that I had always suffered in France. What a joy to have found a country with which I could fully identify and whose culture I now thirsted to assimilate.

At the end of this first stay in Israel in late August, I returned to the port of Haifa to re-embark aboard the Moledet. I remember the boat leaving at dusk. Leaning on the rail in the setting sun, it was with tears in my eyes that I saw Haifa recede and watched her lights beginning to come on. My heart was heavy, full of those recent memories that had moved me, still imbued with the summer scents of the kibbutz. I saw the faces of these young girls of oriental beauty, so different physically from all those I had known in France. My imagination was filled with an exoticism that intoxicated me. I was now convinced that the only possible future for me was in the Jewish state. But I had as yet no clear idea of how to find or create the conditions to make this happen.

This situation was not helped by the fact that I had a contract to resume work with my earlier employer in Strasbourg upon my return to France. I had signed the contract thinking to gain experience in export techniques and felt bound to honor the contract. Also, since I really didn't know anyone in Israel, other than the few acquaintances that I made at Kibbutz Houlata, I wanted time, perhaps a year or two, to devise a plan for how best to consummate my Aliyah. So, I moved into a studio with a bare minimum of conveniences, an apartment near my new employer in Les Mureaux, a dismal working-class city in the suburbs 35 km west of Paris. The fall and then winter weather only added to the loneliness and sadness of my new neighborhood, abetted all the more by the terrible atmosphere I found in my new place of work. All this prompted a quickening of my rapprochement with Israel. Nothing and no one, not even my parents, could keep me in France any longer. The prospect of building a bourgeois Jewish existence no longer interested me. Nor did any of the countless young French Jewish girls that I had met either in Strasbourg or Paris, attract me in the slightest. By contrast, Israel attracted me powerfully because she met the needs of my emerging identity as an "unashamed Jew". Despite the many major challenges that this attraction might impose, I was now free and ready to leave as soon as the opportunity arose. It was even more important now to consider how to create such an opportunity?

I had no desire to contact the Jewish Agency again, but it occurred to me to put myself in touch with Israelis of my generation, preferably students in Paris. With their help, I hoped to find the Israeli professional contacts necessary to arrange for my Aliyah. I knew of Monday student meetings in a Jewish community center on Boulevard Poissonnière. Thew prospect of meeting Israelis, once again hearing Hebrew and being able to talk about this country whose first contact had indelibly marked me... made the 70 km round trip to the community center that first evening not only tolerable, but negligible. Those trips took me to the only beacon of light in the otherwise dreary existence that I was leading at Les Mureaux. The professional, emotional, intellectual nothingness I was feeling became a formidable motivation pushing me towards the destiny which awaited me in Israel. All I needed was a trigger to propel my flight. This presented itself on March 12, 1966, in a most attractive way.

That evening, at the community center in the middle of a meeting of Israeli students, one of them gave a speech frequently interrupted from the listeners in the audience. Of course, I did not understand a word of it, but I quickly re-familiarized myself with my first comforting impressions of the Hebrew language, even tinged, as it was, with a polemical tone. I patiently waited for the end of the speech, which was to be followed by music and dance. While waiting, I noticed just sitting in front of me, a girl with a ponytail and a boy speaking French. Expecting most of the audience to be Israeli, I told myself that, being French, these two must have been lucky to have understood what the speaker was saying. The formal meeting finally ended, someone put on a record with tangos and slow dance music, and the boy in front of me left to go and talk to a friend he had just spotted. Certain that I would be dealing with a Frenchwoman, I leaned towards the young girl to ask her if she would accept a dance. I would have preferred an Israeli dance partner, but as the saying goes, "for lack of thrushes we eat blackbirds"! The girl looked at me quickly and said "Yes", in perfect French, with no foreign accent!

As we began to dance, I asked her to explain the speech we had just heard, admitting that I did not speak Hebrew. I also told her that I had come to these Monday evening meetings wanting to be with young Israelis. The speech "was of little interest," she said. When I told her of the deep impressions left from my first stay in Israel the previous summer, she became more attentive. "What do you do in Paris?" she asked. "I am a sales manager in the export department of an industrial company". "And it pays well?" "Enough to keep me alive" I replied, thinking "Ah, those French Jews, always interested in material things! At that moment, because of her European dress (a plaid skirt and bodice so different from the casual blue jeans and checkered blouses worn by the few Israeli women that I knew), I asked her "Are you English?" "No, I'm Israeli." That response came as a surprise! "How is that? You speak impeccable French and..., you seem to me so different from all those Israeli students, all wearing the same Israeli jeans! "I have lived in Paris quite a bit and I appreciate fashion." I looked at her, moved by a small but sudden surge of interest. She, Israeli, yet so European - is it possible...?

I resumed: "You probably recently immigrated to Israel?" She replied right away, with a certain pride: "I was born there!" Ignore what she read on my face at that moment; I tell you that the dance partner that I took for an uninteresting Englishwoman, was transformed in the blink of an eye into a gift from heaven, suddenly adorned with all the attractions of Solomon's Bathsheva, albeit fashionably attired! I asked her "What attracts you to Paris?" She said, "This city hides so many cultural treasures that I didn't have time to discover during my previous stay." "How long had you lived here the first time?" "Three years, time to complete my secondary studies and pass my philosophy baccalaureate". My amazement grew: a French-speaking Israeli so invested in French culture. My word, here before me was the person I wanted to meet most in the world! I don't remember now if, at the time, I recited any lines from my favorite poets. All I know is that a current was flowing. I was hooked, enthralled..., and I must have looked it. Very quickly, too quickly alas, the companion with whom she had arrived at the club, came back to tell her that he had to leave. I had already forgotten him. Her boyfriend, no doubt or, worse, her fiancé ("the devil take him!"). I resigned myself to seeing my beautiful dream set adrift. However, just before she left, I thought to say: "I very much enjoyed chatting with you and I wish you an excellent stay in Paris, goodbye Miss..., by the way, I am Jacques. "I'm Sarah." "Goodbye Sarah." "Goodbye Jacques." And she walked away.

I watched the exit door close behind her and her companion. I remained, in a pleasure cloud, trying to relive the moments just passed. After less than a minute in this reverie, the door opened, and Sarah reappeared. I thought she had forgotten some personal effect, but no. She walked straight towards me with a smile and said to me: "It would be a pleasure to see you again if, on your side, you also want it". I replied without hesitation: "Yes, of course, that would make me immensely happy". "I'm here on vacation and I have barely a week left before my return." "Well, let us waste no time; tomorrow night if you agree." "Well," she replied, "you could come pick me up from the friend who is staying with me. She is Jacqueline Reznik and she lives at 13, rue Rambuteau, on the 1st floor. 7 p.m., is that good?" "Okay for 7 p.m., I'll see you tomorrow night, goodbye Sarah." And she left. I couldn't believe my eyes or my ears (or my other senses for that matter). So, what had happened to make her retrace her steps to offer me this unexpected new meeting?

That week, we met every evening plus a Saturday and Sunday. Of all these meetings, one especially stays in my memory, and for good reason. After attending a show, we were enjoying a coffee at the Maison du Café on the boulevard des Italiens. The conversation was alive and fluid, that current obviously still flowing between us. In our brief acquaintance, I felt a true attachment to Sarah, feeling a happiness I had never experienced before. I told her so. Then, seized with a sudden inspiration, I added: "How about we stay together?"

I do not remember her reply but, given the time that has passed, it is likely that she did not reject me outright! *Au contraire*, I even believe that on that evening, I called Lyon to tell my parents of our decision, with Sarah beside me. I introduced her to them on the phone. I imagine that they were quite far from sharing my enthusiasm, upon learning that their dear son, however adult and vaccinated, could bond on a whim to a passing stranger from a foreign country, and about whom they knew absolutely nothing.

I remember droving home to Les Mureaux that night that I was talking aloud to myself in the car, saying: "You are crazy, what did you commit to? Who is she anyway? You do not really know her? That does not make any sense, be reasonable...!" But of course, I did not wish to be reasonable. An opportunity had just presented itself for me to break with a universe that I rejected. I no longer wanted a stereotypical "empty" life in France, conforming to a predictable pattern, with no surprises, with no challenges. Now I wanted Israel with all my strength. I felt dimly aware that this country would offer me the best of therapies to cure this disease of Galut, the diaspora. I thirsted for my identity, the only possible identity that recognized my origins. Sarah was the bridge offered by Providence ,finally, to reach the only goal worthy of my interest.

Alea iacta est, "the die is cast"! I had just crossed a Rubicon and was ready to pay the price demanded by this new challenge. Two months later I was in Israel to meet Sarah's family. There were her parents, Ephraim and Tova Ronel, a lovely couple, originally from Austria, who welcomed me warmly as their future son-in-law. Sarah's paternal grandparents, both survivors of the Shoah (about which I knew so little at that time) were there. I especially remember Sarah's grandfather to be a man of great kindness. Sarah, (whom everyone called Sarik) had an older brother, Ami, who was seven years older than she, and a younger sister, Dorit, seven years younger. As I could not speak Hebrew, I spoke with her parents in German, a language I knew as a child and had partially recovered by having studied it in high school. This stay was devoted to visiting various members of the family, and of course, to preparations for a wedding. This was, finally planned for October 1966. We were so happy to be together, Sarik and I, on the dawn of a new existence. For me, my two-fold happiness was to marry the young girl I loved, and to settle in the land of my dreams.

It wasn't long before reality brought me back to earth. Fired by my employer in Les Mureaux, I at once looked for a new job in Israel, but without success; the country was in a deep economic recession. My father quipped with a typical disdain: "He wants to get married, and he doesn't yet have the slightest situation!" Pressed by urgency, I redirected my job search to France and took first placement offered me in the town of Romans sur Isère. This was a serious error of judgement, not to mention a waste of time; we spent our first year of marriage in this uninteresting town.

In May 1967, a political and military confrontation began between Israel and Egypt, Jordan, Syria, and Lebanon. Sarik and I feared the worst and begged Ephraim and Tova to send Dorit, Sarik's younger sister, to us for safety. They refused, probably anticipating the dazzling denouement of this conflict. The Six-Day War of 1967 ended... well..., in six days and in a decisive Israeli victory. This was of course a great relief to Israel and to us. We decided then and there to leave France for Israel; we saw no future other than in the Jewish homeland. The war and complete Israeli victory unleashed an unprecedented wave of solidarity across the Jewish world. Forty years have passed since. Like Edith Piaf, I could sing: *No, I regret nothing, no, nothing at all, no, I don't regret anything, neither good nor bad, all that doesn't matter to me...* You can sing along with Mme. Piaff in French or English at:

Piaff-Non, je ne regrette rien  or,

Piaff-No, I regret nothing

To be honest with you, my readers, the price was steep, but all things considered, it was worth it. I would have blamed myself all my life if I had not begun this crazy adventure. I left feathers here and there and yes, and even almost all my hair, and your mother was not always at the party either, my dear children. There were a few connecting hyphens between us but also so many differences, notably our parental, social, and cultural framework, in addition to the differences of character. Yes, this quarantine union is truly a miracle; it is undoubtedly our real merit, to have resisted, against all odds, all storms, hurricanes, and earthquakes that battered the frail skiff of our family unit. Both being in love with the Paris we had adopted without realizing it, the Latin motto: *Fluctuat nec mergitur* ("It floats and does not sink"). Yes, in the end our frail skiff held out for forty years without sinking.

The conclusion of all this? But of course, it's you, Tamir, Yaron and Assaf, and then your own children. It is thanks to all of you that, on a whim, a gamble if you like, by Sarik and me…, that we won the bet of our lives. In time your children will know that the miracle of *their* lives arose from that earlier one that happened on the evening of March 12, 1966, in a Jewish community center in the middle of Paris. It was then two young people, twenty-seven and twenty-two years old, one French and in love with Israel, the other Israeli and in love with Paris, met and made the wild decision to get married after having dated for only a week (driving their own parents at first, equally crazy). Now we wish for you that the lucky star that guided us on this rugged forty-year life journey…, to wish that this same star will accompany you in turn.

My Time with the BSEL, 1968-1985

BSEL is the acronym of the *Beit Shemesh Engines Limited* factory, founded in 1968 (near the town of Beit Shemesh) to manufacture spare parts for *Turboméca* engines. The parent company was in France, in Bordes, a town in the Pyrénées Atlantiques department near the Atlantic Ocean and close to the Spanish border. It was a French Jew originally from Poland, Joseph Szydlowski, who made the decision to create the BSEL. He was an engineer, inventor, financier, manager, in short, the universal brain of Turboméca. The company that he had founded on the eve of World War II had boomed in the 1950s with the development of an aircraft engine, revolutionary at the time, based on rotary fuel injection. This engine, like all the other engines that came after it, was named after one of the neighboring Pyrenean mountains, in this case Marboré. The famous French *Fouga Magister* training plane was equipped with the Marboré engine, making Turboméca's fortune from the start. At this time, when Israeli-French relations were at their zenith, the Israeli Air Force bought this aircraft. Taking advantage of its excellent maneuverability, Israel converted it into a combat plane. Over time, Turboméca continued its focus on the design and manufacture of small engines for helicopters, leaving the field of large engines to another French company, SNECMA.

On June 3, just two days before Israel's lightning victory over Egypt, Syria and Jordan in the Six Day War, President General de Gaulle of France turned its back on Israel. To win Arab friendship (and of course, access their oil), he decreed an embargo on arms shipments to the Middle East, including cancelling an Israeli order of 50 French Mirage jet fighters. Since Israel was the only country in the region to which France sold arms, this hypocrisy meant that France was cutting off much needed military aid to Israel, just as the surrounding Arab states were threatening her annihilation. This decision was most serious since Israel had built its air force exclusively on French equipment. The French decision thus deprived Israel of the spare parts for the operation of its equipment. Deeply shocked by this treachery, Joseph Szydlowski decided that, since he was unable to deliver spare parts for Marboré engines, it was time to set up a branch factory in Israel. After the anguish Sarik and I experienced during the weeks of waiting before the Six-Day War, this decision coincided with our own to come and live in Israel despite its economic recession and unemployment. Near the end of July, Tova and Ephraim came to visit us in France. Ephraim then declared: "After this resounding victory, there is no doubt that Israel has gained ten years of peace at least". At the time, we wanted to believe this. But those ten years were reduced to seven with the Yom Kippur War in 1973. My in-laws greeted our decision to join them philosophically. As for me, I knew that

I was finally going to realize this dream of coming to live in a country that would truly be mine.

The Jewish Agency organized our voyage to Israel for November of 1967. While awaiting our departure, we spent a week's vacation with Ephraim and Tova in Sweden, and then, set out to Denmark to visit their friends Izi Doroth, his wife, and Carmela Zabine. Among the group was Karl Jespersen., a building contractor and the owner of *Modul Beton*, a company with a patent in modern pre-stressed concrete panels. *Modul Beton* had given an Israeli company, Haran, the license to manufacture prefabricated buildings using its panels. Ephraim and Izi were both shareholders in the Haran company. Jespersen had invited us, at his expense, for a week's visit to his huge countryside property.

After the holidays Sarik and I began preparations for our emigration trip to Israel. Ephraim had already sent us a newspaper clipping in September, reporting the news that Joseph Szydlowski would set up a branch in Israel. I quickly contacted Mr. Szydlowski by phone. As I recall it, here is the conversation that took place:

"Hello Sir, my name is Jacques Lévi. I am twenty-eight years old, preparing to do my Aliyah in Israel and am interested in working in your future branch."
"What is your profession?"
"I graduated from HEC, so I have a background in business administration. I'm ready to come to Bordes for an interview."
"That's not what I need at all. I'm looking for turners, grinders, millers, in short, skilled workers."
"Listen, sir, I'm going to Israel anyway. I'm sending you my CV for your convenience. Maybe you will use it."

Since I said I would do so, I mailed him my CV, convinced by our brief exchange that nothing would come of it. In November 1967, Sarik and I embarked aboard the Moledet ship bound for Haifa, our hearts full of hope for a new existence in the land of my dreams. My father-in-law had bought an apartment for Sarik a few years earlier in the Kirone district of Kiriat Ono, an eastern suburb of Tel Aviv.

Since Ephraim had partially financed this apartment with a mortgage loan, we hastened to replace this loan with the much more favorable loan, one that is granted to any new immigrant by the Jewish Agency. While waiting to move in, we took up residence with my in-laws at 115 derekh Hashalom in Tel Aviv. Sarik started looking for a job as a French teacher, which she quickly found at the Ben Zvi High School in Givatayim.

Two days after our arrival in Israel we were surprised by a visit from the newly appointed director of the new Turboméca branch in Beit Shemesh (provisionally called Turboméca-Israel). He introduced himself as Aharon (Oleg) Nachshon, a recently retired army colonel. He was tall, with hands like paddles, and spoke no French! He told me in English that he'd received my application from Joseph Szydlowski. Mr. Nachshon asked me what position, given my training, I thought would suit me best. I told him that I wanted to learn some Hebrew before taking any post in Israel, and we agreed that we would reconnect after I left the Ulpan (the classic Israeli school for accelerated Hebrew learning for new immigrants). The next day I became a boarder at the Ulpan at 131 Haméginim Avenue in Haifa, there to learn the basics of the Hebrew language in five months. As Sarik had already taught me many grammatical concepts, I was enrolled in the most advanced class. Every Shabbat I spent the weekend with the Ronel family who cheerfully checked to see if I was making good weekly progress. The mood at the Ulpan was even more euphoric, as the country was celebrating our fast Six-Day War victory.

A very popular song from this time was "Yerushalayim shel Zahav" (*Jerusalem of the Gold*), sung by Shuli Natan and composed by the famous Naomi Shemer. Hear Shuli Natan sing it at:

[Shuli Natan-Jerusalem of the Gold](#)

As luck would have it, this song had been composed for a Festival of Song to be held on May 15, 1967, well before the

Six Day War. The enthusiasm aroused by Israel's victory and the reunification of Jerusalem, symbolized by this song, was so great that it triggered in the Jewish communities of United States and Europe an unprecedented wave of investment in Israel. In a few months the country passed from a deep economic recession to a potent economic boom that quickly absorbed the many thousands of unemployed in the various branches of the economy.

I remember, despite the joy and promise of the moment, during a visit to an employment agency, the employee told me after reading my CV: "Your future employer will need a strong Zionist motivation to hire you because you have no specific profession." Unfortunately, this was true, but I was ready to do anything to carve out a place for myself in the country's economy.

In April 1968, with some rudiments of Hebrew, I got down to drafting a job application to *Beit Shemesh Israel Ltd* (BSEL), the subsidiary of *Turboméca Israel*. As promised, I reconnected with Oleg Nachshon. This is how I became one of the first six employees of a company in my new country. From this nucleus, BSEL grew. eventually employing nearly 500. With the factory under construction, the BSEL team was confined to a few offices in Beit Shemesh. Every day I made the round trip from home to Beit Shemesh, in all 100 km. BSEL had hired me at a starting salary of 1,200 Israeli pounds. This was not much but allowed a better subsistence since I was exempt from income tax as a new immigrant.

Our new home at 71 Tsahal Street was a three-room apartment on the 1st floor. This was good because this 5-story building had no elevator. On the other hand, the apartment was above a passage that ran from one side of the building to the other. Because of the flow of winter air through the passage, our floor was always cooled, making it difficult to heat the apartment in winter. We lived there a few years before buying a more spacious apartment at 79 Tsahal Street. This purchase, like that of our final apartment, at 85 Hagalil street, was the impetus of Sarik. I must acknowledge that Sarik functioned as the locomotive in almost all areas of housing and home management.

We had married in late 1966 and two years later Sarik agreed to become pregnant with our first child. On May 6th, Tamir was the result! Sarik entered the Tel Hashomer Hospital on the night of May 5. Unlike more modern days, it was not customary in the 1960s for a husband to keep his wife company in the clinic..., so I was sent home. The next morning around 6 a.m. I awoke to a phone call where a female voice announced: "Congratulations, you are the father of a son!" Still asleep I mechanically replied, "Thank you!" And fell asleep again. Moments later I awoke abruptly to rush to the clinic to kiss Sarik and the newborn.

In the meantime, BSEL was growing and had organized itself into different departments. The company assigned me to the purchasing department because they realized that that my perfect French should enable me to manage orders for the mechanical equipment that was to come from France to Israel. In the hierarchy of BSEL my supervisor was a particularly surly and tyrannical lieutenant-colonel who made my work more difficult.

Oleg Nachshon, aware of this tension but wishing to keep me because of my status as a new immigrant, decided to appoint me as "BSEL representative" at the Bordes de Turboméca plant to resolve any "on the spot" communication problems that arose between Israeli and French technicians. I was a great success in this position because of my excellent relations with French employees and my persistence in solving the technical problems down to the last detail.

As in the past in Strasbourg, I was totally independent, and this also suited me perfectly. Of course, this job did not prepare me for the day I returned to Israel, as you will read.

Sarik, Tamir and I moved into a comfortable French apartment Pau in February 1970. Tamir was nine months old. He was a beautiful baby who filled us with joy. Little by little he learned to walk, then to speak. Looking back on this time, I admit that I did not appreciate enough the gift that was Tamir. I found his presence natural but unremarkable, even though this was not so in the least!

Physiologically he was from Sarik and me, but in truth, he was a divine creation. I think that, to his credit, Tamir was a much better father to his son Eyal than I was to him. Somehow, I had internalized the rigid paternity of my own father, which I have already professed and from which I suffered as a child. I think that Tamir survived *my* parental faults.

For three years we happily lived the best of our remaining youth in Pau, I thirty and Sarik at twenty-five. This region of the western Pyrenees is exquisite, with its green valleys and mountains, and its reputation for fine gastronomy. It was in all ways a prolonged "cure" by way of tourism. Sarik and I learned to ski at Gourette and La Mongie. My parents visited us several times, staying at a local hotel. They adored Tamir who constantly surprised them with a lively and precocious intelligence. Locally we made friends in the small Jewish community of Pau, especially with the Lucien Madar family. On the Turboméca side, we were friends with Robert and Simone Laspuertas and family. In 1972 we enrolled Tamir in the neighborhood nursery school, but he was not happy there, rebelling against excessively rigid rules under which I knew, children could not thrive. I remember a class photo in which Tamir wears a frozen face. I recall one visit of my parents that triggered a health problem for me. This is what happened. One morning I walked to the hotel. As I walked up the stairs to their apartment, I found my father lying unconscious on the stairs. Distraught, I thought he was dead. When I touched him, he suddenly "awoke" and came to himself. It was from this episode that I learned that Dad occasionally passed out. Then, a few days later, the nervous shock I had experienced triggered a delayed rash on my face and limbs. It turned out to be psoriasis, which quickly disappeared from my face, but remained for years especially on the legs.

Sarik, keen to progress in her teaching profession, enrolled at the University of Pau. When she earned her master's degree in French in 1972, she told me then that she had nothing more to do in France. She wished only to teach in Israel. I could have extended my tenure as "BSEL representative" by seven years (this position lasted that long!) had it not been for Sarik's wish that our son Tamir should grow up Israeli. I agreed with her, knowing full well that the price of my return to BSEL would be high. Leaving Pau, I lost my access to a real ivory tower with a unique status. Oleg Nachshon appreciated and was pleased with my work as "BSEL Representative" in France, but he was mindful of the professional qualifications needed at BSEL, that I lacked. Therefore, he appointed me to be "Secretary General" in Israel, an honorary position with job description only vaguely related to the work of BSEL, and that reported directly to the Director General.

We returned to Israel at the beginning of 1973 to the immense joy of Tova and Ephraim, since Tamir was their only grandson. Then on July 13 of the same year on my own thirty-fourth birthday, Yaron was born, a new source of joy for us. Sarik returned to the Ben-Zvi high school where she quickly rose to the post of assistant director to Pnina Bar Sever, the director. This appointment was due to Sarik's strong personality, a trait she inherited from her father, and one that influenced our relationship as a couple.

As I already wrote, all household management decisions were Sarik's. It was convenient for me to let her decide the sale and purchase of our apartments, our cars, and our furniture. Our flat at 85 Hagalil Street in Ganei Tikva bears her hallmarks down to the last detail. Where I expressed myself best was with our three sons (Assaf having come to us in 1977). I often walked with them looking for turtles in the vacant lot that skirted the other side of the Tsahal street. At night, while they were in bed, I would read to them or simply tell them fairy tales. My life with them as children was the epitome of happiness.

The year 1973 took a dramatic turn on October 6, with the outbreak of the *Yom Kippur War*, an event that truly deserves its own chapter. As I had been away from Israel for over three years, I was not reinstated in the army, and so, did not take part in the war effort. Jean Benoit Picard, a BSEL comrade and a new immigrant like me, originally from Strasbourg, was on the Suez Canal during the Egyptian aggression and was sadly, killed. It feels like it was my fate, once again, to survive by remaining outside the conflict.

Albeit at great cost, we won this war too. The BSEL company provided me with a decent salary for almost seventeen years. But the company did not prosper in the end. To the contrary, the two directors placed successively at its head failed to make the business profitable. In the end, Joseph Szydlowski sold it to the State of Israel. In 1985 a third director was appointed with the task of carrying out a massive dismissal of the staff. Financial incentives eased the departures, including mine. During all the time I was with BSEL, I was a quite ordinary employee of the company. Nothing in the positions I held deserves a place among my more vivid memories. This is how, with some reluctance, my career at BSEL ended.

So Many Wrong Moves in My Personal Chess Game, 1961-1986

This chess game began with the choice to enter the HEC. This led to graduation without a well-defined profession. Some people become accountants, dentists, doctors... others become mechanics, plumbers... By training, they develop the know-how to earn a living providing a service, the usual path to success, a healthy family life and self-image in our society. I never had professional training and so... no profession. My parents gave me the chance to study first in high school and then in the HEC, whose national prestige should have opened the doors to a bright future. But not so for everyone, and predictably not so in my case. The HEC was more suited to personalities with business acumen or sons of entrepreneurs, who with or without an HEC diploma, would in the end, carve out a comfortable and secure place for themselves. Although my modest gift for modern languages is a useful tool in the world of business, there was a gift missing in my personality, missing from my business toolbox, one that is essential to create true businessman. The HEC claimed to provide solid general notions of accounting, law, and political economy, professions best solidified by family and social connections! The HEC never claimed to provide academic programs to train specialists in these disciplines. So, I graduated with poor job prospects, pointed in a direction that was not mine..., an obvious and serious disadvantage.

I fault the HEC for not warning inexperienced students like me not to place too much confidence in the employment prospects its diploma might promise. Some less naïve classmates at the school, aware of the insufficiency of training, simultaneously pursued studies of law or accountancy. For me however, the HEC was a "lark's mirror", an attractive but useless, shiny thing. It is ironic and a puzzle to me that long before entering the HEC competition, I took psychotechnical tests designed to guide me in the most suitable directions based on my talents and personality. Clearly the tests were either poorly designed, or their results were badly misinterpreted. The tests, intended to help young people avoid future ineptitude and failure, had failed me.

Now, knowing myself a bit better, I'm sure that teaching, social work, or even the theater would have suited me better than the business world. My mother had the foresight to see in me the qualities of a teacher. But I had a strong prejudice against the teaching profession: to me, a teacher had a hard job, was often heckled for doing it, and as civil servants, were not especially well paid. So, I ignored my mother's nudges in this direction. In any case, my father would rather have seen me in an accounting apprenticeship instead of wasting time and family funds on what he thought to be fruitless studies. One thing is certain: I entered professional life without any relevant training, in short without a profession. This was a mistake with serious consequences to my career and my psyche.

After graduating the HEC in 1961 at age 22, I began my 18-month military service in the French army. I finished as a corporal in 1963 and started as sales manager in a company in the steel trade in Strasbourg. I stayed for two years as *first assistant* to the sales manager who had hired me. But he quickly saw that I lacked authority and thus was not suited to a hierarchical position (i.e., to be a "boss"). Somehow, I created an independent department by and for myself, buying and selling preformed "cold sections" (steel formed into different shapes by rolling and bending, rather than by heat and molding).

I managed to develop an honorable turnover, but nothing more. Call this another mistake.

In 1965, because I could speak both English and German, I thought I would do well when I moved on to a company in the Paris suburbs that manufactured and supplied those *cold sections*. There I became an assistant in their Export Department. Alas, I did not impress even myself in this job. I was clearly not cut out for "doing business". I should have faced reality then and there and moved on in another direction. Yet another error in judgement.

The year 1966 was marked by the three life-changing events I already described: I met Sarik in March, we married, and we decided to start a new life in Israel. This of course was in no way a mistake! But when the recession raging in Israel forced me back to France, hurriedly I took a job with a company in Romans sur Isère to promote the sale of shoe polish. This was a product I should have known was only marketable with large-scale publicity, something that this company could not afford. Of course, another serious error in judgment on my part; after a few months I quit.

This coincided with the political crisis that developed in the run-up to the Six Day War in June 1967. Sarik's and my anguish were such that we decided to leave France for Israel for good and there, to look for a job that better suited my personality. It was then, before we could implement this decision, that Ephraim Ronel my father-in-law whom I called Aba (Dad in Hebrew) intervened in my personal "march to destiny", suggested that reach out to Joseph Szydlowski. As you read earlier, He was just opening BSEL (Turboméca's Israeli branch) to get around the French embargo of equipment sales to Israel, and so began the seventeen-year career as a buyer at BSEL. During that time, I held various positions. I am the first admit that in none of these did I distinguish myself. However, traumatized by my earlier failures in France, I clung to this job for fear of risking unemployment yet again. I had resigned myself to being just an employee, nothing more. I fooled myself into thinking that I could survive like this until retirement. At least, I thought, I would have had a livelihood that allowed me to feed my family.

This way of thinking was another mistake. It was plain enough to me that I was not a success in Sarik's eyes. I'm sure she had resigned herself to being married to this low-level employee. I was the opposite of my father-in-law, brilliant and successful in all his endeavors. Sarik and I were far from being a happy couple for years. I keep coming back to the fact that my consolations were my sons, Tamir, Yaron, and Assaf, always a source of joy and pride to me.

No matter how much I questioned myself, to guess what special gifts I had that would finally get me out of this state of mediocrity, I saw not the slightest solution. Succeed... I was dying to, but at what? I wanted, indeed would have to be, less afraid, more enterprising, more creative, more daring. But to become this alternate person, I would have had to unearth abilities buried in my subconscious. Alone I might have taken risks. With a wife and three children, it was too much to ask. Again, I paid dearly for this paralysis. The massive 1985 layoffs at BSEL were made only a little more bearable by the severance pay (required in France).

Now at the advanced age of forty-six, I tried my "luck" with the French subsidiary of an Israeli metal machining company, hiring on as sales director in the village of Ungersheim (Alsace, department Haut-Rhin). I should have known from all my previous business "adventures" that I was in for another failure, another dismissal, and a bitter disappointment for Sarik. She had hoped because of my new situation, to remain in France. This time I confronted my employer, strongly opposing his ultimate dismissal decision. Nevertheless, destiny decided in my fate when at the industrial tribunal I was overruled. I left Ungersheim deeply discouraged and went to Lyon to see my parents, hoping to find some moral support. Quite the opposite, my father greeted me with bitterness, rightly (in his view) noting: "So what was the point of those studies at the grand École des Hautes Études Commerciales de Paris (HEC)?" Suddenly I felt completely foreign to this house where I had lived my childhood. As for my ever-hopeful mother, she told me to keep my head high. So, without work and with my head as high as possible, I returned to Israel. When I arrived, I was welcomed by Sarik who, with the *coup de grâce*, brutally informed me: "I do not at all want to feed the unemployed!" Clearly in my desperation, I had made another mistake. As it happened, before leaving for France, I had done quite well on another of those psycho-technical tests, this one offered by a textile company that manufactured nylon thread. On my return to Israel, they hired me. But it turned out that after only a few months, I was once more on the wrong track. You could say that my future was once again, hanging by a thread...

The Miracle of the KKL, 1987-2002

In 1987, I was already forty-eight years old. All those mistakes, especially the last two in just two years was too much. Not only was my morale low, but my image within the family was even lower. To be an unemployed husband is not a good state of affairs. Conjugal feelings fare poorly during this sort of ordeal, and in the eyes of Sarik, whose father was the very symbol of success in all that he did, I now appeared, less a "head of the family" and more like the perfect "failure". To top it off, we were heavily in debt with a mortgage on our apartment at 85 Hagalil Street. How would we deal with the relentless deadlines for payment? The horizon of our existence had suddenly become terribly dark. Once again, I had to run to the employment office, start interviews again, but this time with two consecutive failures in my CV. More than once I felt overwhelmed by despair.

One day when I was walking along Hagalil Street, where we had lived for five years, I heard, through the lowered window of a car door, a Hasidic song. It rang in my ears as an encouragement not to despair. The words in Hebrew are:

"רבי נחמן מברסלב כך אומר:
אסור להתייאש!
ואם הגיע זמן קשה –
רק לשמוח יש!"

In English, "Rabbi Nahman of Bratslav said: One should never be discouraged and, if trials occur, then one should rejoice". I was not at all religious. I did not practice any of the mitzvot and limited myself to the renewal of *Yom Kippur* once a year. Believe me, in my misery, I found that the words of this song settled like a salve over my tortured mind. They brought me a consolation that no one near to me was of a mind to give. I have never since forgotten this moment, this instant when an unexpected ray of hope shone on me. I felt somehow reassured even if, unlike the last line of this stanza, I did not exult in joy.

One evening (perhaps this same evening) passing by Aba, my adopted stepfather, who was perfectly aware of my moral distress and who knew me well, handed me a job offer that he had cut from the newspaper, telling me: "Here is work that should fit you like a glove!" The clipping advertised the position of *Delegate for Legacies and Wills* in the French office of the Keren Kayemeth LeIsrael, or KKL (in English, the JNF, or Jewish National Fund). The job requirements were that candidates have good "people skills", a university background, some understanding of legal matters, and a solid knowledge of the history of the Jewish people. As Aba said, this offer was tailor-made, a gift from Providence and finally, a path out of the damned world of commerce and business. I at once sent my application, On December 6, 1987, I received a telegram from the JNF to appear for an interview at the Jerusalem office on Wednesday December 9.

This is how I got to know Avraham Shaar, director of personnel, and Fred Bleiman, the titular *General Delegate* in Paris. Bleiman was to complete his mission at the same time as the current *Delegate for Legacies and Wills*, Zvi Lamdan. Naturally, I was not the only candidate in the running, but I felt that the impression I left on these two people was quite good. However, they gave me to understand that, in any case, the choice of the future *Delegate* should have the OK of the President of the JNF of France in Paris, Edouard Colin, a French Jew, a lawyer, and a well-known personality in Zionist circles in Paris. He was however, reputed to be very difficult to deal with. The position was to be filled next summer and I would have to submit once more to a series of psycho-technical tests and interviews over the next 6 months. Of course, I felt that this work would indeed suit me perfectly, but nothing, absolutely nothing, guaranteed that I would get this job.

Destiny now put me to a new test, the last, but a large one. During the first psycho-technical examinations carried out within by a specialized institution outside the JNF, I found myself in competition with several candidates. These examinations may have been ordered by more than one employer, so I could not know if I had one or more competitors for the JNF position. I remember well one of these candidates who it turned out later, was such a competitor, and who was hired into the JNF post I wanted. That candidate, a little older than I, was Itzhak Baro. Among all the candidates, he stood out for his conspicuous behavior. During the breaks between two tests, while we were among candidates in the cafeteria, he spoke loudly, always on the slightest pretext, mostly to brag. I later learned that he was well known to Aba from a time when they had been assigned abroad together in government service. Aba, who was his superior, was not happy with Baro's performance and sent him back to Israel.

Jumping ahead a bit, I have to say that, against all odds and unbeknownst to him, Itzhak Baro played an unexpected and decisive role in my eventual success with JNF. Here's how. The tests to which the candidates were subjected included comprehensive medical exams. I had noticed that Baro was abnormally short of breath. This must have shown up in his medical exam and prompted the JNF doctor to look for the reason for this shortness of breath. Whatever the cause, a *Delegate for Legacies and Wills* must be physically fit to run all over Paris to visit the testamentary candidates. And travel by the metro (underground, subway) involves innumerable descents and ascents of long, steep stairways that would be very difficult for a man in Baro's physical condition. The JNF management must have known this very well and, despite this crippling handicap and against all logic, Baro was hired as the Delegate. As it happened, less than six months later, Baro underwent serious surgery that ended his mission. If Baro was hired in this position despite his physical handicap, I figured that the JNF had given in to political pressure. So, if my psycho-technical and medical tests raised no red flags, my candidacy would nevertheless have been rejected in favor of Baro. In the end, a cynical choice that did little honor to the JNF leadership, sent me back to the ranks of the unemployed.

But this denouement was temporary! With yet another trick up his sleeve, Destiny wanted the JNF to fill a second position in France, that of *General Delegate* of the Paris Office, which had opened upon F. Bleiman's departure. This was of course a hierarchically superior position. The candidate originally chosen had to abandon his selection due to illness. I believe that the good results of my psycho tests had perhaps justified Avraham Shaar to consider me for this position, even though I had not applied for it. Indeed, I knew that this was a position at the top of a hierarchical ladder that I had not duly ascended, having been denied the opportunity of the ascent; I should first have gained experience as a *Delegate for Legacies and Wills*. And even beyond the missed opportunity, bitter experience taught me that I was not made to lead people or manage conflicts. However, I felt for obvious reasons, and despite dark forebodings, that I had no other choice but to accept the position, hoping that once in France, things might work out for themselves. But they did not.

Edouard Colin was feared by the Jerusalem leadership. An unbearable dictator, he had already caused the hasty departure of a prior *Delegate General* and very likely contributed to Fred Bleiman's (his successor's) heart attack. My chances of professional survival with a person like this were zero at best. How was I to defend the interests of the JNF of Jerusalem if I did not dare to challenge M. Colin. I was guaranteed dismissal at the first confrontation, an impossible situation bordering on the absurd. What can one possibly say about an organization, the JNF, that delegates its responsibilities to an employee knowing it is unwilling to support this employee in any dispute with President Colin?

The fact that the JNF of France was legally independent of the JNF in Jerusalem just highlights the absurdity of my situation, even though the two organizations supposedly serve the same cause, pursuing the same objectives. Thus, it was no surprise that eight months after I took office, Colin demanded my dismissal from the JNF in Jerusalem…, and the home office complied.

But before I received yet another 'pink slip', it was my luck that at this time, Itzhak Baro proved to be an unsuccessful

Delegate for Legacies and Wills, with a total absence of financial results during the few months of his service. His mission ended following a heart attack and convalescence from surgery. He returned to Israel around March 1989. I was still in the position of *General Delegate*. In that role I requested the provisional recall of Zvi Lamdan, Baro's predecessor, who had done especially well in his mission, bringing in substantial funds to the JNF. (By the way, I already knew Zvi who lived in my neighborhood in Israel; some twenty-seven years later in 2015, his widow Nelly became my partner a few months after my own widowhood, another of Destiny's tricks).

In my office in Paris on May 11, 1989, I took the phone call that was my 'pink slip'. On the other end of the line Avraham Shaar informed me that the Management, based on the complaints of Colin about me, had decided to appoint in my place a new *General Delegate* in the person of Dan Nahmias, the brother of David Nahmias, one of the directors of the JNF in Jerusalem. The call was not a total surprise, given the state of permanent conflict that I endured with Colin and the resulting tensions between me and some other elements of the personnel in the Paris office. But I did not imagine that the home office would take such a decision without having heard from me beforehand. That day, Sarik, a hundred leagues from suspecting the roof that had fallen in on our heads, called to say that she was about to buy tickets for a show. When I told her what had just happened, I heard abrupt silence. There was no longer any question of a show.

The shock of my dismissal was very painful. Three big failures in less than four years were worse than "too much" to bear. Once again, the sky darkened so much that I did not see any salvation. Coming back to Israel after less than a year would prove to the family and everyone else that Jacques Lévi was just a failure, collecting failures, unable to fit into a profession even for which exams and tests had otherwise foretold success.

With heavy hearts we had to take all material measures to return to Israel: to give the owner of our apartment notice, to sell the car that we had just bought, to pack our personal effects. Again, I started writing CVs, including to French companies, which, if hired, would have meant a breakdown of our family life.

Four days after my dismissal, just for the sake of form, I wrote a letter to the President of the JNF, Moshe Rivlin, asking him to reconsider his decision. It was in vain. My morale could not have sunk lower. As soon as I had the chance, I unloaded on Colin in a tone that betrayed my anger, reproaching him for the desperate situation in which *he* had put me. I made it clear that he was responsible for the serious professional and material damage that this dismissal caused me. I must have pricked his conscience: He wrote to Avraham Shaar stressing the point that the position for which I had applied was that of *Delegate for Legacies and Wills* and in fact, not *General Delegate*, with the result that the JNF had not really given me a chance to prove myself. What happened next happened quickly.

On June 22, I addressed a new letter to Moshe Rivlin, a real indictment against what to me was a glaring injustice. On the same day, Colin proposed to Avraham Shaar by telegram that I be appointed to take charge of the now vacant post of *Delegate for Legacies and Wills* and for which, he repeated, I had applied. On Sunday, June 25, a holiday in France but a workday in Israel, there unfolded a real drama, one worthy of a movie contract! Sarik, Yaron, Assaf and I were in the apartment sadly busy packing our belongings for our return to Israel when the phone rang at noon. "Hello Jacques," said Abraham Shaar's voice, as if speaking to the camera, "How are you?" "As good as the present circumstances allow," was my reply. "We received your last letter as well as that of M. Colin. Would you agree to be our *Delegate for Legacies and Wills*?" I was stunned..., speechless. Sarik, who was plugged into the earpiece, whispered urgently: "Say yes, say yes!" I finally reacted and like an automaton that can only articulate in a neutral tone, saying "Okay." "Well," said Shaar, "I will confirm this by fax. You will finish transmitting your duties to Danny Nahmias and you will take the instructions from Zvi Lamdan to start your new duties. Good luck!" I put the phone down, not yet taking in the full measure of what I had just heard, of this reversal of fortune. A guardian angel was perhaps aroused by the prayers my mother told me that my father said every night in on my behalf. Did my father's prayers put an end to the series of trials and setbacks that I had endured these last three years, throwing me a providential lifeline and protecting me from a real shipwreck? The JNF offer and my acceptance were the beginning of successful professional career. All that remained was for me to prove that the choice of the JNF had been justified. I was going to use this chance with all my strength. I could not know it then, but my destiny had just taken a 180 degree turn and made a "loser" a "winner".

Given the turmoil we had just gone through and the instability of my situation, Sarik and I decided by mutual agreement that in the interest of the education of Yaron, aged sixteen and with two years of the bac coming up, that it was better that she returned to Israel with him and Assaf leaving me alone in Paris. This was also in my own interest because I would be able to devote more of my time to restoring the damaged department of *Legacies and Wills*, so thoroughly undermined by Itzhak Baro's incompetence. I would have to regain the confidence of those testators and investors that he had neglected so seriously. Assaf, who was 12, was not happy at having to leave Paris. The city had thoroughly seduced and intoxicated him, something any Paris lover can understand. I asked him the reason for his enthusiasm for this city. He thought a moment and then in French, said to me: "It's special". Of course, I had to agree!

This reversal of fortune coincided with the end of the school year and the start of the summer vacation. We took advantage of a commission given me by the JNF of France, to meet some Parisian retirees, themselves on summer vacation. This allowed us to enjoy ten days together before I would be separated from Sarik, Yaron, and Assaf. Back in Paris, Sarik dictated to me in a notebook that I have kept to this day, the main recipes that allowed me to cook basic and substantial cuisine. We baptized this document "my survival notebook". I had just celebrated my 50th birthday. Only then was I able to "take flight" towards a professional development that I could not have imagined. I often relive this near miracle of my life because from that moment, how I appeared to my family and social entourage and even more so, to myself, changed completely. Like a plant long deprived of water and is finally watered properly, I was about to straighten up, see the sun, and come back to life and color.

I will not recount the stages of my new work which led me from success to success and made me one of the best Delegates for Legacies and Wills in Europe. Simply put, I underwent a psychological metamorphosis when I regained a self-confidence that my earlier failures had undermined. The management of the JNF in Jerusalem now treated me with consideration in light of the brilliant financial results which I accumulated over the months. It was a sweet revenge on the past. It was time. The situation of our household had been ruptured, cracked to a danger point, but not yet beyond repair. *Now*, finally, my family was reassured: I was not a real "failure".

Dan Nahmias himself, seeing me accept 'demotion' to a position quite subordinate to his own, at first considered me with some reserve. But later, he stepped back from his first judgment and in his turn expressed his esteem. In fact, we even became great friends. It is also true that since he came into office, he had been able to see just who Colin was. The first clashes between the two did not take long. This time, there ensued a real Jewish war, fought by lawyers and ending in breakup of the Jerusalem and Paris JNF offices.

Having written this far, I realize now that this account of my years with the JNF is not complete without another professional confession and its denouement. The confession is related to a personality trait: my inability to speak in public. Indeed, I lived the first fifty years of my existence with the certainty that I was totally incapable of expressing myself in public. I would panic in fright over public audiences of any more than three people. Years earlier, when I was working as the general secretary of the BSEL, I was asked by management to address a group of young Air Force officers in a conference room, to give them an overview of the factory, its history, and its production capacity. I knew this information well but the idea facing thirty of these officers was so frightening that I asked a colleague, a reserve officer, to replace me.

Even though I knew the subject much better than my stand-in, I suffered in silence while he revealed more of what he did not know than what he did. I could do nothing, convinced that I had no other choice than to let him speak.

When I was appointed *General Delegate* of the JNF, it was made clear to me that I would have to speak in public before the communities of France. So, I reluctantly resolved to do so by reading carefully prepared addresses written in advance. I also became the subject of interviews in the studios of Jewish radio broadcasts in Paris and in the provinces. This was a real ordeal, accompanied by violent, emotional cold sweats. The studio was a small room with a table in the middle where the interviewer sat with the interviewee. Through a glass window overlooking a room where the program coordinator was, I had to be attentive to his signal to start, which also resulted in the lighting of a red lamp above the table. I had to go through several interviews before I could pass the red lamp test. I managed, but the breakthrough only came later, after I became *Delegate for Legacies and Wills*.

I thought that to help me in my prospecting of co-religionists without children (we called them audiences "of the 3rd age"), I could appeal them by speaking to them on subjects of Jewish history. I believed that by thoroughly learning a given subject I would not find it so hard to speak without anxiety and without a prepared text. My first lectures were far from being exemplars of oratory, but over time, with experience, and by dint of reflections and constant self-criticism, I improved my technique. Then..., one beautiful day, I realized that the stage fright was gone. What a great joy to know that I could speak easily in public and moreover, that I was listened to with interest. I naturally took some pride in this discovery, and great pleasure knowing that I had managed to free myself from obstacles considered insurmountable for so many years.

I remained with the JNF for almost thirteen years. I served as *Delegate for Legacies and Wills* in France for about six years, from 1989 to 1995. At the end of this mission, the JNF expressed its satisfaction by committing me to service in Tel Aviv for three more years, in which time my replacement in Paris was Maurice Kagan. At his departure, I resumed service as *Delegate for Legacies and Wills* in Paris for about another two years until October 2002.

About My Work as a KKL Delegate for Legacies and Wills

As a KKL Delegate, I was charged to find elderly French Jews without children wherever they were, to meet with them and to convince them to put the KKL (the JNF) in their wills and testaments. Nothing could be less simple than soliciting old people for donations, and precisely because they are old, to draw their attention to the fact that they will disappear one day soon, and that, for this reason, I am asking them to think about the future of their wealth and heritage. To understand by which mental process an elderly person comes to the decision to write (or change) their will, I had to find out whether such a person was one that survived the Shoah, whether he or she was a remnant of the Jewish population having lost many family members. Then I had to show and persuade them that the only hope of a better future for this battered fraction of the Jewish community lay in the land of Israel. Into this role I brought a remembrance (not always welcome) of physical and moral scars of the near-death experiences common to all these survivors. 90% of them came from the countries of Eastern Europe, especially Poland, but also Romania, Hungary and Czechoslovakia. Yet each of these Jews knew that in the absence of a will, their heritage would end up in the hands of the country of their residence, in this case France. Once reminded of this and of the active role taken by France in the implementation of the Shoah, they were keen to prevent rewarding her, in fact rewarding a criminal state with their legacy. The need for a will in favor of an Israeli organization then became obvious.

Finally, there remained the choice of the beneficiaries in Israel. Though I represented the KKL, there were still other worthy Israeli institutions interested in such precious legacies, starting with the State of Israel represented in Paris by its Embassy and which benefited from most of the Jewish heritage. Added to this there were also the United

Jewish Appeal, various universities, and Israeli hospitals and the Weizmann Institute. This is where my personal story came in, thanks to which I gained the trust and often the affection of these Holocaust survivors. For more than one of them I was the missing son or the one they never had. With a testament favoring the KKL they favored me as well.

To sum up, my professional career was mediocre for a long time until I reached the summit, my time at KKL. Thanks to this, my self-image, and my image in the eyes of those close to me, finally became positive. As I already noted, I owe to my work at KKL the discovery of a real hidden talent as a public lecturer. After retirement, this led to a second career that I have enjoyed to this day. Of course, I can never forget that it is to Divine Providence that I owe this momentous turning point in my life.

Since 2002 and My Pilgrimage in France, May 2011

I have been a retiree now for more than eighteen years, using the skills I developed as a *Delegate for Legacies and Wills* to lecture about Jewish history in Israel. My audiences are mostly French immigrants, of which there are many. It has been my pleasure to learn and speak on such topics as the history of the Protocols of the Elders of Zion, Zionism, and Israel in general.

It was during this period that I also had the time to revisit and begin recording my own recollections. I have already covered most of them in this memoir, but they are worth summarizing here. They include: my attendance in 2007 at the ceremony in Corsica honoring among the *Righteous of the Nations* one of our saviors, Louis Milelli; a 2011 visit to the grave in Catalonia of Dr. Bénet, the *hero of the resistance* whose 'false papers' saved us in St. Antonin Nobleval; regular visits to St. Antonin, especially to my "adopted sister" Collette; and the passing of Sarik in 2017. In 2011 I also began a friendship with Christian Didier, of whom I will write in the next chapter.

Here I want to add that it took me until 2010 (at age 71) to devote time to remembering Josef and Grete Isaac, my maternal grandparents. I realize that I had occupied a big place in their lives, in the short period that was left to them. Even so, I had devoted little thought to them in my own life. I do have the privilege of being a grandfather and watching my grandchildren grow up, but I never had the privilege of growing up with my own grandparents near on both sides. I never had the chance to know the affections of grandparental indulgence or to benefit from their attention, patience, wisdom, and love, which would have been freely given. With these would have come the gift of listening, this attention, patience and love of listening that seem so often lacking in parents caught up in everyday exigencies of life. The time had come to repair, to close this loophole as best as possible.

My grandfather Josef Isaac (59 years old) and the author (3 years old) in the summer of 1942; In six months, Joseph will be deported from Drancy in 'convoy 50' on March 4, 1943

All of my remembrances begin with the photo that you see here. It is of mediocre quality, but it is a last document in which my maternal grandfather Josef Rudolf Isaac appears with his hand on my head, as if to bless me. It must be from 1942. So, I'm about three years old. It was probably taken with a very simple camera, that of a neighbor or a friend perhaps. We will never know. As I appear in bright light, Josef's gaze is in the shadow of his hat. I can tell where his eyes are. The expression is infinitely sad because his situation has become so precarious.

In this spring or summer of 1942, he is a 59-year-old man, shattered by Fate. He has lost everything: the homeland that rejected him and that humiliated and totally despoiled him, then the loss of his wife who died a year earlier in terrible suffering caused by a widespread cancer, and in the end, the loss of all his fortune. At that moment he is nothing more than a destitute refugee. He was plagued by a stomach ulcer, surely triggered by anguish at the deadly threat to the Jews of Europe. In a few months he will be deported and assassinated in the Majdanek death camp. Germany, his homeland for generations, not only denied him his homeland, but has been working since the Wannsee Conference in January 1942 to engineer his demise. He very likely learned through rumors from the *occupied zone* of France that Jews of both sexes, of all ages, of all origins, were being conveyed in appalling conditions to an unknown destination in the East, and that this cannot bode well. Night and day, he must have wondered what will become of him, of his only daughter Hilde, of his son-in-law Walter, of his only grandson Jacky..., when he knows that Hitler's anti-Semitic fury of extermination knows no rest, no limits. Could it be that he wondered if we would all soon disappear?

In this first half of 1942, the German armies are victorious on all fronts, going from conquest to conquest. Almost all the countries of Europe are under their control. Even the Soviet Union is on the verge of collapse. Josef's despair is, alas, well justified. Maybe he would have heard the news of the German surrender at Stalingrad on February 2, 1943, while still in Gurs camp. It might have been a supreme, last consolation before his transfer to Drancy and a month later, his deportation by convoy 50 of March 4, 1943, to Majdanek to be gassed. Having reached an age that Josef and Grete were not blessed to reach, I strongly felt the need to identify with what they lived in the last years of their existence and, more particularly, in France where they thought to find refuge, only to find death instead, I undertook this trip to France to go to the different places where they stayed until their last station in France, Dijon, for Grete who died there of generalized cancer in 1941 and, Drancy, the collection camp north of Paris, from where Josef was deported.

My pilgrimage arises from these memories, remembered, received, and imagined. Let me begin with my time in Charente where my grandparents, Josef and Grete Isaac, stayed in the village of St. Genis d'Hiersac after their evacuation from the Moselle. They stayed there from September 1939 through the summer of 1940 before coming to Dijon where my mother and I (just one year old) were living. Also, after evacuation from the Moselle, Josef's sisters, my great-aunts Caroline Bender (with her husband Julius Bender) and Johanna Samuel, came to St. Amand de Nouère. They lived there from September 1939 to October 1942, until they were arrested by the French gendarmerie, then taken to Angoulême, transferred to Drancy and from there, deported to Auschwitz.

I arrived in Angoulême on the afternoon of May 16, 2011, where Mme. Michèle Gaillard, the mayor of St. Genis d'Hiersac, gave me a warm welcome. She had managed to free herself between two meetings just to meet me at the train station. We agreed to meet the next day with the Piquet family (Adèle Piquet hosted Josef and Grete about seventy years ago) and the family of Arlette Dulac, the eighty-year-old neighbor of the Piquet family who remembered Josef and Grete Isaac well. Jean Michel Urbajtel, of the small Jewish community of Angoulême, met me at the Terminus hotel, opposite the station. He had been warned of my arrival by Gérard Benguigui, president of the community, whom I had contacted from Israel. Jean Michel took me to dinner at his home in Brives, a suburb of Angoulême, where his wife Patricia and his sister-in-law Jacqueline, from Paris were waiting for us. I was then invited to have lunch with them the next day, before our departure for St. Genis d´Hiersac, where I met Arlette Dulac and Christine Rodriguez, the great-granddaughter of Marguerite Elisa Piquet who had taken in Josef and Grete. Mayor Michèle Gaillard, with Arlette, Christine (and her husband Alfred Rodriguez), Jean Michel and another woman from the community of Angoulême, had organized a small party at the town hall for me so that I could meet the people and their descendants who had welcomed my grandparents.

To conclude this brief chapter, I want to salute the remarkable work of memory carried out by Gérard Benguigui. He saved from oblivion the tragedy experienced by 442 Jews rounded up in Charente on October 8 and 9, 1942, interned in the Philharmonic Hall of Angoulême for eight terrible days, and then being shipped like cattle to Auschwitz via Drancy. At the end of his research and after a long struggle with an obstinate French administration, he obtained the necessary authorizations and succeeded, on October 8, 2012, seventy years after the tragedy, in inaugurating a giant commemorative plaque on which are inscribed the names of the 387 deportees of this roundup and of the 23 *Righteous of Charente* (recognized at Yad Vashem) who put their lives in danger to save Jews.

Gérard Benguigui, President of the Jewish Association of Angoulême

My Friendship with Christian Didier, 2011-2015

Although I grew up and lived in France until I made Aliyah to Israel at the age of 27, I had never heard of René Bousquet nor fully understood the extent of France's responsibility for the deportation of its Jews. Around me, no one spoke of it. My awakening really started with an interview with Louis Darquier de Pellepoix, which appeared in L'Express on 11/28/1978.

In May of 1942, Pellepoix, a virulent anti-Semite, had been appointed in 1942 to head the *Commissariat Général aux Questions Juives* (General Commissariat for Jewish Questions). The Commissariat had been established a year and a half earlier to issue the anti-Semitic Vichy laws. At the time of the interview, Pellepoix, himself a refugee living in Spain, revealed René Bousquet's direct responsibility (as the Vichy chief of police) for the deportation of most of the 76,000 Jews of France. After an 'automatic' conviction as a Vichy official in 1949, Bousquet (officially the *general secretary to the police for Vichy France*) was given a reduction in sentence and then in 1958, amnesty. Living now with total impunity, Bousquet had had a comfortable career in banking since 1943, ran (unsuccessfully) for political office after the war, and remained involved in politics through the 1980s, enjoying a golden retirement in Paris with no remorse. In Paris in 1942, Bousquet's second in command of the *French National Police* in Paris was Jean Leguay. On July 16 and 17, Leguay organized the *Grande Rafle du Vel' d'Hiv* (the grand Vel d'Hiv Roundup), the mass arrest of 13,000 Jews. He first detained the Jews in the Vel' d'Hiv ("winter stadium") in Paris, then transferring them to Drancy and other French concentration camps, from where they were deported to the death camps of eastern Europe. After the war, Leguay escaped any charges and instead became president of the Warner-Lambert pharmaceutical company (that later merged with and became Pfizer).

In 1979, following the interview with Pellepoix, renowned Nazi Hunters Serge and Beate Klarsfeld launched legal actions against Leguay and Bousquet. Legal procedures against Leguay dragged on for ten years when in 1989, he died of cancer, escaping justice, unpunished. During the same decade, Bousquet war activities were subject to further investigations and accusations. In 1990, L'Express published a new report entitled *Investigation of a Forgotten Crime* that revealed to the general public Bousquet's own role in the *Vel d'Hiv* Roundup, as well as in the internment of Jewish mothers and their children in the Pithiviers and Beaune-la-Rolande camps, and the forced separation of these mothers from their children. The prior deportation of the mothers was at the urgent request of Vichy to the Germans; that of the children came a few months later. At long last in 1991, the French Ministry of Justice indicted Bousquet for his role in the Vel d'Hiv Roundup. While the trial of the German Klaus Barbie was settled in three years, proceedings against the Frenchman Bousquet dragged on for four years until June 8, 1993..., when it was definitively interrupted with his execution by a man called Christian Didier.

I was then in Paris on behalf of Jewish National Fund. I believe that the political will of the time was to bury Vichy crimes at any cost and that Bousquet's crimes would not to be brought to light in a spectacular trial. Bousquet, and thus France's *guilt-by-collaboration*, would go unpunished. This, despite the fact that Bousquet himself boasted of it shamelessly in an interview by *L'Express* a few months before his death. Equally shameless, this article was only published, but only after Christian Didier's *act of justice*.

Christian Didier

Eloquently titled *Death of a Collaborator*, this 4- or 5-page article did not mention Christian Didier's name even once, a fact that speaks volumes about the stubborn French *omerta* about the Vichy period. It does not surprise me, because the facts clearly show that the Jews of France have never been, are not, and could not ever be fully French. This is still the reality, one that will be hypocritically denied but is the reality that underlies all my correspondence with Christian Didier. Indeed, the Jews of France, although holding French nationality, are not in my view considered equal in status to Auvergnats, Bretons or Alsaciens, whether by politicians or by the average Frenchman. On the political level, de Gaulle's remarks on the Jews during a press conference on November 27, 1967, attest to this: Jews are a "people" (therefore to be distinguished from the French people), "elite, confident and domineering". Likewise, the comments of Raymond Barre after the attack on the Copernicus Synagogue on October 3, 1980: "This hateful attack was meant to strike Israelites going to the synagogue, and it struck innocent French people crossing the rue Copernic". This implication of "Israelite" guilt could not be a slip of the tongue from a head of government. The comparison made in the statement was either carefully crafted, or reflective of a deeply held belief that Jews are different from true French people. Such remarks explain a posteriori why the organizers of the Pétain and Pierre Laval trials, did not allow facts into evidence of the 76,000 Jewish deportations from France. Since the Jews could not axiomatically be genuine French, these deportees could not be brought up among the charges leveled against French people in these trials. In this light we can better understand why René Bousquet did not worry that in his 1949 trial, he might be found guilty for most of the Jewish deportations. The deportations were not addressed at the trial. In fact, they were not addressed in the decision of the High Court of Justice of June 23, 1949.

The active complicity of the Vichy collaborators in the deportation of the French Jews from France was never spoken of at the time (it was in fact concealed) by all post-war French governments until an address by President Jacques Chirac on July 16, 1995…, fifty years after the end of World War II, and two years after the execution of

Bousquet. This was a first step taken towards recognition of Vichy complicity, but this complicity itself has never the subject of a proper Vichy trial. From such a trial, all France would have finally learned in great detail what happened to their Jewish "compatriots" under Vichy, and who was responsible. It is not too late for such a trial. It goes without saying that a "proper Vichy trial" now cannot seek justice, but would be exclusively didactic, with the goal of exposing to the nation once and for all, its long-hidden truths.

It should be clear that these truths must be incorporated into the history of France, to be taught to the younger generation. France must demand this trial of her wartime political power as the best, if not the only way to honor her lost Jews and her Jewish Community. The goal of justice was the goal of the Klarsfelds for so many years, carried out by Serge Klarsfeld, President of the Association of Sons and Daughters of Jewish Deportees from France. It began with the ten-year investigation of Jean Leguay until his death without trial, and of his superior René Bousquet that ended with his execution without trial by Christian Didier. Klarsfeld must have realized soon enough that he was tilting against windmills. Bousquet, during his lifetime, described him in an article in L'Express as "agitated".

I undertook my 2011 pilgrimage to honor the memory of my maternal grandfather, Josef Rudolf Isaac. He had been arrested in Lyon (still in free France) in September 1942 by the French police of Vichy, interned successively in the French camps of Rivesaltes, Gurs, and then Drancy, before being deported to Majdanek where he was murdered. For part of this pilgrimage, I took the entire route of his "Stations of the Cross" in France, following his expulsion from Germany. It was then that I finally realized the extent of the suffering he had endured, both physical and moral. And it was then that I understood the deliberate, violent justice given by Christian Didier to the unpunished René Bousquet. I clearly saw his act as a timely reminder that France had failed in its duty to justice. What no French Jew who survived the camps had dared to do, Christian Didier, who is not Jewish and did not have to suffer from Bousquet, did. This is why I decided in 2010, very late, to personally express to Christian Didier my admiration and my gratitude for having avenged the suffering, deportation and killing of my grandfather Joseph Rudolf Isaac.

For five years I kept up a friendly correspondence with Christian Didier until his untimely death on May 15, 2015. Likewise, I tried in vain, to demand a review of Christian Didier's trial with a view to his acquittal, or at least, a pardon. All the major figures in the Jewish world turned their backs on me as they turned their backs on him during his 1995 trial when he pleaded for their help. I am left to say, on behalf of all of the 76,000 Jewish victims of Vichy in general, and on behalf of my grandfather Josef Isaac, his two sisters Caroline Bender and Johanna Samuel as well as his brother-in-law Julius Bender, blessed forever the memory of Christian Didier.

Questions for Discussion of *From Vichy to Jerusalem*

1. Jacques originally wrote his memoir for his three sons and his grandchildren, but when he shared it with a few others, they suggested that his story would resonate with a wider audience. Do any parts of Jacques' autobiography resonate with you? Which parts, and why?

2. How would you describe the differences between daily life before the Lévi family went into hiding and after they were living in St. Antonin Nobleval?

3. Thinking about those *Righteous Among the Nations* (recognized at Yad Vashem or not) without whom the Levi family would surely have perished, why do you imagine that they would take such risks to protect the Lévis?

4. Is there someone in your life that you think (or would like to think) would be your Marcel, Milelli, Bénet, Gracia, willing to risk their lives to protect you from the hatred of others? Is it difficult to explain or imagine such a person? Why or why not?

5. Jacques might describe his relations with his father as *fraught*, and yet he seems to have borne him no less love. In what ways, positive or negative, did Walter affect Jacques' growing up, both in hiding during the war and post war?

6. Jacques' post-war years in school in Lyon are a mixture of encouraging and discouraging times. How would you describe the good times and how might they have they influenced his feelings about France? If they were conflicted feelings, do you think they were resolved, and if so, how?

7. Growing up after the war, Jacques seems to have defined and redefined, or at least evolved his ideas about success in life. Why do you think this is?

8. Jacques ascribes his long-delayed success in life to fate, or destiny. What does Jacques mean by fate? Do you think "life lessons" are what we call fate?

9. Emile Zola wrote *J'Accuse* in 1898, taking French antisemitism to task over the Dreyfus affair (*L'Affaire Dreyfus*). Jacques accuses France of an antisemitism that she never admitted, much less renounced, an antisemitism with which she has never come to terms. What did this memoir teach you about antisemitism in France? Is it different than your understanding of antisemitism in Germany?

10. How did you (do you) react to the last chapter about Jacques' correspondence with Christian Didier, the man who shot René Bousquet, a police official of the Vichy regime?

11. What technologies available to Jacques and his family that enhanced life, or made it more bearable in the period before and during WWII? How do you think today's technologies would have changed Jacques stories of the 1930's and 1940's, if he had access to them?

12. Have you heard or read other first-person stories of people who survived the Holocaust or is the child of a survivor? What is similar about this story? What is different?

INDEX

2
23 Righteous of Charente, **132**

3
3 Musketeers, **61**

9
99th Infantry Regiment, **23**, **25**

A
A Good Little Devil, **63**
Achard, Amédée, **60**
Ajenstat, **97**
Aladdin and the Magic Lamp, **61**
Alain Janconesco, **81**, **82**, **84**
Alain Resnais, **39**
Alfred Hitchcock. *See* Hitchcock, Alfred
aliyah, **98**, **100**, **101**, **108**, **132**
Allied air force, **72**
Allied forces, **13**
Allies, **18**, **22**, **32**
Alsace, **17**, **33**, **117**
Amalthea, **75**
André Daubard, **75**
Angoulême, **9**, **131**, **132**
Annonay paper mill, **45**
Anschluss, **3**
anti-Semite, **20**, **63**, **133**
antisemitic, **2**, **14**
Appendicitis, **89**
Arandon, **13**
Ardèche, **45**
Arlanc, **20**
Arthur Rimbaud. *See* Rimbaud
Aryan, **6**
ashamed Jew, **99**
Assaf, **106**, **113**, **117**, **123**, **124**
Association of Sons and Daughters of Jewish Deportees from France, **136**
Auschwitz, **19**, **57**, **83**, **131**, **132**
Austria, **2**, **3**, **104**
avenue Berthelot, **19**
avenue de Clichy, **95**
Avenue de Saxe, **51**

B
Baccalauréat, **88**, **90**
Bad Dürkheim, **8**
Baden, **17**
Bambi, **61**
Bar Sever, Pnina, **113**
Barbie, Klaus, **19**, **27**, **134**
Bar-Mitzva, **12**, **63**, **77**
Baro. *See* Baro, Itzhak
Baro, Itzhak, **120**, **121**, **124**
Barre, Raymond, **135**
Bastille Day, **55**
Baudelaire, **83**, **85**
Baudelaire, Charles. *See* Baudelaire
Beaune-la-Rolande, **134**
Bécassine, **61**
Beit Shemesh, **106**, **109**, **110**
Beit Shemesh Engines Limited, *See* BSEL
Belgium, **13**
Ben Zvi High School, **109**
Bender, Caroline, **131**, **137**
Bender, Julius, **131**, **137**
Bénet, Paul Marius, **34**, **35**, **41**, **128**
Benguigui, Gérard, **131**, **132**
benschen, **6**, **7**
Ben-Zvi high school, **113**
Bergman. *See* Berman, Ingmar
Berlin, **18**
Bertrand Cerf, **96**, **97**
Besson, **59**
Big-Bill the breaker, **61**
birkat hamazon, **6**
Bizet, Georges, **62**
Bleiman, Fred, **119-121**
Blum, Albert, **65**
Blum, Delphine, **66**
Bobin, **75**
Bogart, Humphrey, **61**
Bonnet family, **89**
Bordes, **106**, **108**, **111**
Bornecque and Cauet, **75**
boulevard Anatole France, **73**
boulevard des Belges, **70**, **73**
boulevard des Italiens, **103**
boulevard Malesherbes, **93**
Boulevard Poissonnière, **101**
Bousquet, René, **132-136**
Bresson. *See* Bresson, Robert
Bresson, Robert, **95**

BSEL, **106-117, 125**
Bugarel, *Alex*, **30**
Bugarel, Alex, **33**
Bulgaria, **40**
by convoy 50, **130**

C

Café du Parc, **79**
Carmen, **62**
Carné. *See* Carné, Marcel
Carné, Marcel, **95**
Catalan, **35**
Cerf family, **95, 97**
Cerf, Bertrand, **97**
Cerf, Juliette, **97**
Cerf, Robert, 96
certificat, **68**
Chalon-sur-Saône, **16**
Chambaran camp, **13**
Charente, **9, 131, 132**
Charlet, Pierrot, **68**, *See* Charlet, Pierrot
Chevalier, Maurice, **54**
Chevallier and Audiat, **75**
chicklets, **58**
Chirac, Jacques, **136**
Christmas, **32, 43, 60, 63**
Clair. *See* Clair, René
Clair, René, **95**
Cleveland, **14**
Clichy metro station, **57**
Colbert, **63**
cold profiles, **116**
cold sections, **115**
Colin. *See* Colin, Edouard
Colin, Edouard, **119, 121**
collaboration, **18, 39, 134**
collaborators, **28, 71**
Collège de Charleville, **86**
comics, **61**
Commissariat Général aux Questions Juives, **133**
compulsory labor service, **28**
Comtesse de Ségur, **60**
concentration camps, **39**
convent in Monplaisir, **21**
Convoy 45, **82**
convoy 50, **129**
Copernicus Synagogue, **135**
Corneille, Pierre de, **63**

Corsican captain, **24, 25**
Cours Vitton, **73**
Curwood, James, **60**
Czechoslovakia, **2, 127**

D

Damia, **37**
das Reich Division, **38**
Daubard. *See* Daubard, André
Davidson, **36**
de Gaulle, Charles, **39, 107, 135**
Death of a Collaborator, **135**
Delegate for Legacies and Wills, **119-128**
demarcation line, **15, 16**
Denmark, **40, 108**
denunciation, **15, 23**
Department of Isère, **13**
deportation, **19, 23, 24, 28, 40, 57, 81, 130-137**
derekh Hashalom, **109**
Didier. *See* Didier, Christian
Didier, Christian, **128, 132-137**
Dijon, **1, 3, 8-17, 130, 131**
Dimet, **51, 52, 53, 59**
Dinky Toys, **68**
Disney, Walt, **61**
Doré, Gustave, **77**
Doroth, Izi, **108**
Drancy, **10, 19, 129-133, 137**
Dreyfus Affair, **83**
Dreyfus, Sam, **79**
Du Guesclin, **63**
Dulac, Arlette, **131**
Dumas, Alexander, **60**
Dumbo, **61**
Dunkirk, **13, 34**

E

École des Hautes Études Commerciales, **57, 117**
École normale supérieure, **87**
Ecole Supérieure de Commerce, **93**
economic recession, **107, 110**
Edith Piaf, **48, 54, 105**
Egeria, **75**
Eisenstadt, **97**
England, **2, 4**
Ephraim, **105, 113**

extermination, **10**, **28**, **63**
Eyal, **111**

F

fake ID cards, **23**
fake military record, **23**
false identity, **19**, **35**, **38**
false military file, **21**
false papers, **21**, **34**, **35**, **128**
fascism, **7**
Fenimore Cooper, **60**
Fernand Raynaud, **83**
final solution, **18**
Flaubert, Gustave, **60**
Flynn, Errol, **61**
forged papers, **19**
Fort Montluc, **19**
Fouga Magister training plane, **107**
Francazal air base, **37**, **42**
Francis Lemarque, **83**
Franck, Charles, **18**, **88**, **89**
Frack, Claude (Claudie), **68**, **69**
free zone, **10**, **13**, **15**, **18**, **23**
French embargo, **116**
French military service, **99**
French Militia, **20**
French Ministry of Justice, **133**
French National Police, **133**
Fuehrer, **12**

G

Gaillard, Michèle, **131**, **132**
Galilee, **99**
Ganei Tikva, **113**
Garnier, Simone, **45**, **46**, **66**
Gaston Cayrou, **75**
General Commissariat for Jewish Questions, **133**
General Delegate, **119**, **122**, **126**
General Delegate of the Office, **120**
genocide, **39**
Georges Brassens, **91**
Germany, **2**, **6**, **9**, **11**, **12**, **18**, **28**, **71**, **130**, **136**
Gestapo, **10**, **19**, **21**, **22**, **24**, **30**, **35**, **36**
Gintzburger, Julien, **79**
Givatayim, **109**
Gourette, **112**

Gracia, **40**
Gracia family, **42-44**
Gracia, Claude, **42**, **69**
Gracia, Colette, **28**, **30**, **41-44**, **128**
Gracia, Hélène, **42**
Gracia, Margot, **28**, **43**
Gracia, Raymond, **28-34**, **41-43**, **93**
Grande Rafle du Vel' d'Hiv, **82**, **133**, **134**
Grange Blanche Hospital, **10**, **21**
Gross Wannsee, **18**
Grünstadt, **2**
Gurs, **17**, **130**, **137**
Gurs internment camp, **17**
Gus and Gaétan, **61**
Guy de Maupassant, **60**

H

Hadar, Shimon, **99**
Hagalil Street, **113**, **118**
Haifa, **99**, **100**, **108**, **109**
Haméginim Avenue, **109**
Haran, **108**
Haut-Rhin, **117**
He Was a Small Ship, **37**
HEC, **57**, **77**, **87**, **92-98**, **108**, **114**, **115**, **117**
hidden Jew, **43**
Hitchcock, Alfred, **95**
Hitler, **2**, **3**, **9-13**, **130**
Holland, **13**
Holocaust, **24**, **128**
Honoré de Balzac. See Balzac
Horvilleur, **82**
Hugo, **60**
Hungary, **127**

I

Identity check, **20**
Il Etait Un Petit Navire, **37**
Ingmar Bergman, **95**
Investigation of a Forgotten Crime, **133**
Isaac, Grete, *See* Oma Grete
Isaac, Josef, **128-131**
Isaac, Josef Rudolf, see Opa Josef
Isère, **13**, **105**
Israel, **2**, **7**, **24**, **26**, **83**, **92**, **97-107**, **118**

Israelite, 53, **64**, 135
Israelite guilt, **135**
Italy, **18**, 26

J

Jacqueline Terrier, **91**
Jacques Brel, **76**
Jacqui Wallon, **30**
Jean de La Fontaine. See La Fontaine
Jean Rendu, **49**
Jerusalem of the Gold, **109**
Jespersen, Karl, **108**
Jewish Agency, **99, 101, 109**
Jewish Association of Angoulême, **132**
Jewish Community Center of Strasbourg, **99**
Jewish Community of France, **83**
Jewish National Fund, See: JNF
Jezreel Valley, **99**
JNF, **119-127**. See also Jewish National Fund
Jordan, **105, 107, 109**
Josef (Rudolph) Isaac, *See* Opa Josef
Jugurtha, **86**
Jules Holtz, **49**

K

Kagan, Maurice, **126**
keepah, **64**
Keren Kayemeth LeIsrael, See KKL
Kibbutz Houlata, **99, 100**
Kibbutz Sarid, **99**
Kiriat Ono, **108**
Kirone district, **108**
KKL, **97, 118, 119, 127, 128**, See: also JNF
Klarsfeld, Beate, **133, 136**
Klarsfeld, Serge, **133, 136**
Koress Leute, **55**

L

L.S. Meyer of Pforzheim, **3**
La Capelle Balaguier, **42, 43**
La Fontaine, Jean de, **52, 63, 85**
La Mongie, **112**
La Rue de Notre Amour, **37**
La Vie en Rose, **48**
Lamdan, Zvi, **119, 122, 123**
Languedoc, **41**
Laocoön, **75**
Lardanchet bookstore, **60**
lark's mirror, **115**
Laspuertas, Robert, **112**
Laspuertas, Simone, **112**
Laval, Pierre, **135**
le debacle, **13**
Le Gaffiot, **75**
Le Galizon, **89, 90**
Le Petit Périgord, **94**
Le petit poisson et le pêcheur, **52**
Leguay, Jean, **133, 136**
Les Amoreux des Bancs Publics, **92**
Les Distribies de Nina, **85**
Les Mureaux, **100-105**
Les Pieds Nickelés, **61**
Lévi ,Pierrot, See Lévi, Pierre
Lévi, Ella, **3, 15, 57**
Lévi, Emilie, See Oma Emilie
Lévi, Fred, **3**
Lévi, Gérard, **97, 98**
Lévi, Hilde, **1, 9, 20, 130**
Lévi, Isaac, *See* Opa Isaac
Lévi, Liesel, **3, 62**
Lévi, Pierre, **69**
Lévi, Richard, **3, 57**
Lévi, Robert, **3, 56,66**
Lévi, Selma, **3**
Lévi, Walter. **1-5, 10-16, 20, 21, 30-35, 130**
L'Express, **133-136**
Liberation, **21, 44, 49**
Liberté, égalité, *fraternité'*, **15**
line of demarcation, **22**
Lino Ventura, **19**
Linz, Robert (Kurt), **79**
Loire, **13**
London, Jack, **60**
Lorraine, **9**
Louis Milelli. *See* Milelli, Louis
Loulou Bonnet, **89**
Lucullus, **6**
Luis Mariano, **42**
lumberjack, **32**
Luxembourg, **13**
Lycée du Parc, **64, 70, 74, 86, 90, 92**
Lycée Edgar Quinet, **90**

Lyon, **10, 13, 15-27, 29-32, 36,40, 43, 44, 48-50, 53-58, 64-66, 71, 89, 92, 93, 95, 103, 117, 136**

M

Mac Miche, **63**
Madame Bovary, **60**
Madar, Lucien, **112**
Maison des Elèves, **77, 93, 94**
Maison du Café, **103**
Majdanek, **10, 130, 137**
Mama(n), see Lévi, Hilde
Mamichou, **50**
Marboré engine, **107**
Marcel Mouloudji, **83**
Marcel, Francine, **31, 35**
Marcel, Jacques, **28, 35, 36, 41**
Marcel, Marie, **14, 29, 66**
Marcel, René, **4, 5, 26-30, 34-36, 40, 66**
Marcel, Sophie, **4, 37**
Marie Wolf. *See* Oma Wolf
Marseille, **6**
Marseilles, **26**
Martin Karcher, **77, 94**
Melville, Jean-Pierre, **19**
Mérimée, Prosper, **59**
metal machining company, **117**
Migdal Haemek, **99**
Mignon, **62**
Milelli, **25, 26**
Milelli family, **19, 25, 26**
Milelli, Louis, **22-26, 128**
Milelli, Pierrot, **26**
Milelli, René, **26**
Milice Française, **20, 23**
militiamen, **28**
Millot, **75, 84**
Ministry of the Interior, **13**
Modul Beton, **108**
Moledet, **100, 108**
Mollard, Marie-France, **48**
Mollard, Marie-Louise, **45, 47**
Montluc, **21**
Montluel
 castle of, **13**
Montplaisir, **18**
Morsbach, **9, 15**
Moselle, **131**
municipal school, **50, 51, 58**

Murel, **36**
Museum of the Resistance and Deportation, **19**

N

Nachshon, Aharon (Oleg), **109**
Nahmias, Dan, **122, 123, 125**
Nahmias, David, **122**
Nantes, **13, 94**
Naomi Shemer, **109**
National Revolution, **15**
Necker hospital, **16**
Nelson, **60**
Nice, **26**
Nightingale of My Loves, **42**
nightmare, **15, 20, 23, 44, 67, 71**
No, I regret nothing, **105**
Non, je ne regrette rien, **105**
Nonorgues, Albert, **30, 38, 39**
Normandy, **38, 44**
North Africa, **18, 22**
Nuit et Brouillard, **39**
Nuremberg Laws, **2**

O

occupied France, **18, 133**
occupied zone, **13, 15, 130**
Oma Emilie, **7, 11, 12**
Oma Grete, **8, 9, 11, 12, 16, 130-132**
Oma Lévi. *See* Oma Emilie
Oma Wolf, **8, 15, 17, 18, 20, 32, 71**
Opa Isaac, **3, 7, 11, 12**
Opa Josef, **2, 8, 10, 12, 15, 18, 21, 32, 129,137**

P

Palais de Justice, **21**
Parc de la Tête d´Or, **46**
Parc de la Tête d'Or, **73**
Parc Monceau, **93**
Pau, **17, 42, 111, 112**
Paul Meurisse, **19**
Paul Reynaud, **93**
Paul Verlaine. *See* Verlaine
Papa, see Lévi, Walter
Pearl Harbor, **18**
Pélisson, Joseph, **20**

Pélisson, Louise, **20**, **63**
Pellepoix, Louis Darquier de, **133**
Perrache station, **19**
Pétain, Philippe, **13-15**, **135**
Pfizer, **133**
Picard, Jean Benoit, **113**
Pierre Charlet, **59**, **67**
Pierrot, **63**
Pinocchio, **50**, **61**
Piquet family, **131**
Piquet, Adèle, **131**
Piquet, Marguerite Elisa, **131**
Pithiviers, **133**
place Bellecour, **19**
Place des Célestins, **18**, **19**, **22**, **25**, **27**
place Saint Pothin, **51**
Ploum ploum tra-la-la, **56**
polnische yiden, **65**
profit motive, **23**
Protocols of the Elders of Zion, Zionism, **128**
Pyrenees, **13**, **17**, **35**, **112**
Pyrénées Atlantiques department, **106**

Q

quai Saint-Antoine, **21**

R

Rabbi Nahman of Bratslav, **118**
racial exclusion laws, **14**
Racine, Jean-Baptiste, **63**
ration cards, **31**, **34**
Red Cross hospital, **89**
Reparations, **71**
Resistance, **19**, **28**, **33-36**, **41**
reunification of Jerusalem, **109**
Rhineland Palatinate, **3**
Rhône, **24**, **51**, **67**
Richelieu, **63**
Righteous Nations Medal, **25**
Righteous of the Nations, **22**, **24**, **26**, **128**
Rimbaud, **85**, **86**
Rivesaltes, **136**
Rivet, **83**, **84**, **85**, **86**, **87**
Rivlin. *See* Rivlin, Moshe
Rivlin, Moshe, **123**

Robin Hood, **61**
Roc d'Anglars, **32**
Rodriguez, Alfred, **131**
Rodriguez, Christine, **131**
Roman, **75**, **85**
Romania, **127**
Romans sur Isère, **116**
Romulus and Remus, **75**
Ronel family, **109**
Ronel, Ephraim, **104**, **107**, **116**
Ronel, Tova, **107**
Rosa, rosa, rosam, **76**
Rouen, **4**, **14**
Rouge et Or, **60**
roundups, **10**, **28**
rue Alphonse Fochier, **19**
rue Alphonse Legros, **1**, **13**, **16**
rue Bugeaud, **38**, **44**, **48-51**, **67**, **68**, **71**, **72**
rue de la Pélisserie, **38**
rue des Dames, **95**
rue Garibaldi, **44**
rue Lécluse, **57**
rue Louis Blanc, **90**
rue Pierre Corneille, **50**, **51**, **58**, **67**
rue Raoul Servant, **64**, **68**, **71**, **72**
rue Verguin, **73**

S

Saint Amand de Nouère, **131**
Saint Basil, **5**
Saint Genis d'Hiersac, **131**
Sainte-Marguerite clinic, **69**, **70**
Samuel, Johanna, **131**, **137**
Samuel, Suzy, **77**
Sand, Georges, **60**
Santa Claus, **63**
Santé Militaire school, **19**
Sarah. *See* Sarik
Sarik, **98**, **104-128**
School of Advanced Commercial Studies, **57**
School of Military Health, **28**
Serge and Beate Klarsfeld, **133**, **136**
Service du Travail Obligatoire, **28**
Shaar, Avraham, **119-123**
Shabbat, **6**, **7**, **109**
shameful Jew, **7**
Shoah, **5**, **39**, **66**, **104**, **127**
Shuli Natan, **109**

Sign of the runway, **60**
Simone Signoret, **19**
Six Day War, **107, 109, 116**
skullcap, **64**
SNCF, **20**
SNECMA, **107**
Snow White, **61**
Sobibor, **10**
Spirou, **61**
St Genis d 'Hiersac, **9**
St. Antonin, **28-33, 35-44**
St. Antonin Nobleval. *See* St. Antonin
St. Genis d'Hiersac, **15**
Stalingrad, **130**
steel trade, **115**
Steinberg , Maurice, **57**
Steinberg , Yvonne, **15**
Steinberg, Armand, **16, 57**
Steinberg, Oscar, **15**
Steinberg, Robert, **16, 57**
Steinberg, Yvonne, **57**
Sternheimer, Ida, **13**
Sternheimer, Renée, **95**
STO, **28**
Strasbourg, **87, 99, 100, 111, 113, 115, 121**
Strauss-Kahn, Dominique, **93**
Superman, **61**
Sweden, **40, 108**
Sylva, Berthe, **54**
Szydlowski, Joseph, **106-109, 114, 116**

T

Tales and Legends, **60**
Talmud Torah, **65, 76**
Tamir, **64, 106, 111-113, 117**
Tarn-et-Garonne, **19, 28, 41**
Tarzan, **61**
Taurynia, **35**
Tel Aviv, **108, 126**
Tel Hashomer Hospital, **110**
Terminus hotel, **19, 27, 131**
terror, **21**
The Army of Shadows, **19**
The Art of Poetry, **85**
The Jewish Agency, **108**
The little fish and the fisherman, **52**

The Lovers Kissing On a Public Bench, **92**
The Six-Day War, **105**
The Street of Our Love, **37**
The White Roses, **54**
Théâtre des Célestins, **63**
Third Republic, **93**
Thomas, Ambroise, **62**
Tino Rossi, **54**
Tintin, **61**
Toulouse, **4, 13, 15, 27-30, 32, 34, 37, 42, 43, 66**
Tova, **104, 105, 113**
Tsahal Street, **110**
Turboméca, **42, 106, 109-112, 116**
Turboméca-Israel, **109**
Turenne, **63**

U

Ulpan, **109**
Ungersheim, **117**
United Jewish Appeal, **127**
United States, **3, 11, 18, 56, 110**
Urbajtel, Jean Michel, **131, 132**

V

Vel d'Hiv Roundup, **133, 234**
Vel d'Hiv, *See* Grande Rafle du Vel' d'Hiv
Verlaine, **85**
Verne, Jules, **60**
Vernet, **50, 51**
Vichy, **5, 10, 13-23, 29-33, 44, 63, 71, 83, 133-137**
Victor Hugo. See Hugo
Villard de Lans, **89**

W

Wallertheim, **8**
Wallon family, **30**
Wallon, Hélène, **20, 21, 30, 43**
Wallon, Jacqui, **43**
Wallon, Louis, **20-22, 30, 31, 34, 35, 43**
Wannsee Conference, **130**
Warner Lambert, **133**
Weizmann Institute, **128**
Winnweiler, **3, 7**

Wizard of Oz, **61**
WIZO, **95**
Wolf, Arnold, **8**
Wolf, Fritz, **8**
Wolf, Marie. *See* Oma Wolf
Women's International Zionist Organization, **96**
Wormser, Albert, **79**

Y

Yad Vashem, **24-26**, **41**, **132**
Yaron, **106**, **113**, **117**, **123**, **124**

Yerushalayim shel Zahav, **109**
Yom Kippur War, **107**, **113**

Z

Zabine, Carmela, **108**
Zany, **56**
Zorro, **61**